topps®
BASEBALL CARDS

White Sox

Text by
Bill Shannon

PRICE STERN SLOAN
Los Angeles

Officially licensed by Major League Baseball

Official Licensee

© 1988 MLBPA
© MSA

An MBKA Production

Printed and bound in Hong Kong.

TEAM LEADERS

Hall of Famers

Luis Aparicio
Luke Appling
Chief Bender
Frank Chance (Manager)
Eddie Collins
Charlie Comiskey (Executive)
Jocko Conlan
Hugh Duffy (Manager)
Johnny Evers
Red Faber
Hank Greenberg (Executive)
Clark Griffith
Harry Hooper
George Kell
Bob Lemon (Manager)
Al Lopez (Manager)
Ted Lyons
Edd Roush
Red Ruffing
Ray Schalk
Al Simmons
Ed Walsh
Hoyt Wilhelm
Early Wynn

Twenty Game Winners

1901 -	Clark Griffith (24)
1902 -	Roy Patterson (20)
1904 -	Frank Owen (21)
*	Patsy Flaherty (20)
1905 -	Nick Altrock (24)
	Frank Owen (21)
	Frank Smith (20)
1906 -	Frank Owen (22)
	Nick Altrock (20)
1907 -	Doc White (27)
	Ed Walsh (24)
	Frank Smith (22)
1908 -	Ed Walsh (40)
1909 -	Frank Smith (25)
1911 -	Ed Walsh (27)
1912 -	Ed Walsh (27)
1913 -	Reb Russell (22)
	Jim Scott (20)
1915 -	Jim Scott (24)
	Red Faber (24)
1917 -	Ed Cicotte (28)
1919 -	Ed Cicotte (29)
	Lefty Williams (23)
1920 -	Red Faber (23)
	Lefty Williams (22)
	Dickie Kerr (21)
	Ed Cicotte (21)
1921 -	Red Faber (25)
1922 -	Red Faber (21)
1924 -	Hollis Thurston (20)
1925 -	Ted Lyons (21)
1927 -	Ted Lyons (22)
1930 -	Ted Lyons (22)
1936 -	Vern Kennedy (21)
1941 -	Thornton Lee (22)
**1953 -	Virgil Trucks (20)
1956 -	Billy Pierce (20)
1957 -	Billy Pierce (20)
1959 -	Early Wynn (22)
1962 -	Ray Herbert (20)
1964 -	Gary Peters (20)
1971 -	Wilbur Wood (22)
1972 -	Wilbur Wood (24)
	Stan Bahnsen (21)
1973 -	Wilbur Wood (24)
1974 -	Jim Kaat (21)
	Wilbur Wood (20)
1975 -	Jim Kaat (20)
1983 -	LaMarr Hoyt (24)
	Richard Dotson (22)

*Pitched with White Sox (1) and Pirates (19).
**Pitched with Browns (5) and White Sox (15).

No Hitters

9-20-02	Nixey Callahan
9-06-05	Frank Smith
9-20-08	Frank Smith
8-27-11	Ed Walsh
5-14-14	Jim Scott
5-31-14	Joe Benz
4-14-17	Ed Cicotte
*4-30-22	Charlie Robertson
8-21-26	Ted Lyons
8-31-35	Vern Kennedy
6-01-37	Bill Dietrich
8-20-57	Bob Keegan
9-10-67	Joel Horlen
7-28-76	John "Blue Moon" Odom, Francisco Barrios
9-19-86	Joe Cowley

*Perfect Game.

League Leaders

Batting Average

1936 - Luke Appling (.388)
1943 - Luke Appling (.328)

Home Runs

*1915 - Braggo Roth (7)
1971 - Bill Melton (33)
1972 - Dick Allen (37)
1974 - Dick Allen (32)

*Played with White Sox and Indians.

Runs Batted In

1972 - Dick Allen (113)

League Leaders

Wins
*1907 - Doc White (27)
1908 - Ed Walsh (40)
1917 - Ed Cicotte (28)
1919 - Ed Cicotte (29)
*1925 - Ted Lyons (21)
1927 - Ted Lyons (22)
*1957 - Billy Pierce (20)
1959 - Early Wynn (22)
*1964 - Gary Peters (20)
*1972 - Wilbur Wood (24)
1973 - Wilbur Wood (24)
1982 - LaMarr Hoyt (19)
1983 - LaMarr Hoyt (24)
*Tied

Strikeouts
1908 - Ed Walsh (269)
1909 - Frank Smith (177)
1911 - Ed Walsh (255)
1953 - Billy Pierce (186)
1958 - Early Wynn (179)

Earned Run Average
1906 - Doc White (1.52)
1917 - Ed Cicotte (1.53)
1921 - Red Faber (2.47)
1922 - Red Faber (2.80)
1941 - Thornton Lee (2.37)
1942 - Ted Lyons (2.10)
*1951 - Saul Rogovin (2.78)
1955 - Billy Pierce (1.97)
1960 - Frank Baumann (2.68)
1963 - Gary Peters (2.33)
1966 - Gary Peters (1.98)
1967 - Joel Horlen (2.06)
*Pitched with Tigers and White Sox.

Most Valuable Players
1959 - Nellie Fox
1972 - Dick Allen

Rookies of the Year
1956 - Luis Aparicio
1963 - Gary Peters
1966 - Tommie Agee
1983 - Ron Kittle
1985 - Ozzie Guillen

Cy Young Award Winners
1959 - Early Wynn
1983 - LaMarr Hoyt

World Series Appearances
*1906   1919
*1917   1959
*World Champions

Club Records

Batting
Runs . . . . Johnny Mostil (135, 1925)
Hits . . . . Eddie Collins (222, 1920)
Doubles . . . . Floyd Robinson (45, 1962)
Triples . . . . Joe Jackson (21. 1916)
Home Runs . . . . Dick Allen (37, 1972)
. . . . Carlton Fisk (37, 1985)
Runs Batted In . . . . Zeke Bonura (138, 1936)
Stolen Bases . . . . Rudy Law (77, 1983)
Batting Average . . . . . . Luke Appling (.388, 1936)

Pitching
Games . . . . Wilbur Wood (88, 1968)
Innings . . . . Ed Walsh (464, 1908)
Wins . . . . Ed Walsh (40, 1908)
Strikeouts . . . . Ed Walsh (269, 1908)
Saves . . . . Bob James (32, 1985)
Earned Run Average . . . . Doc White (1.52, 1906)

Compiled by Bill Haber.

1952

Having introduced the "Go-Go Sox" to the South Side of Chicago the previous season, manager Paul Richards' second year at the helm produced an identical 81-73 record but another step up in the standings from fourth to third. Without any .300 hitters and only one 15-game winner (lefty Billy Pierce, 15-12), the performance was remarkable. After a slow start the Sox started rolling in June, winning 24 of 34 games in one stretch into July to hold second as late as July 11. Then came a rugged eastern swing that produced 9 losses in 10 games and eventually a slide into sixth before a strong finish earned the Sox third place.

Second baseman Nelson Fox and first baseman Eddie Robinson were the top hitters (.296) with Robinson hitting 22 homers and producing a club-high 104 RBIs. Minnie Minoso (.281) also had 22 stolen bases to go with his 13 homers. Joe Dobson (14-10), Saul Rogovin (14-9) and Marv Grissom (12-10) were other winning pitchers.

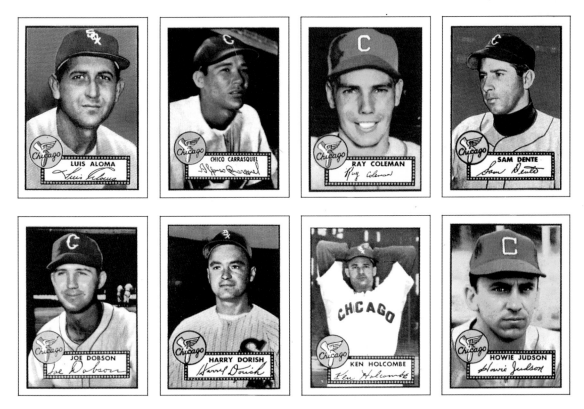

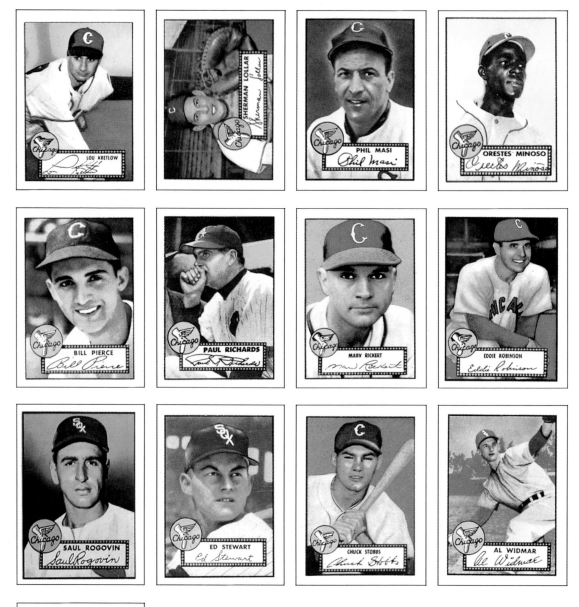

1953

A winning record in every month except September (11-13) enabled the Sox to finish third for the second straight season, 11½ games from the league lead. A 20-10 July was the hottest part of the season. The final record was 89-65. Minnie Minoso soared to .313 with 15 homers and a team-high 104 RBIs while Nelson Fox hit .259 with a surprising, career-high 72 RBIs. Short-stop Chico Carrasqual batted .279 but Ferris Fain, a two-time batting champion acquired from the Philadelphia A's, was a major disappointment. Fain broke a finger in an Aug. 2 fight and ended up hitting only .256 with 6 homers and 52 RBIs.

A more successful deal was the one on June 13 that brought Bob Elliott and righthander Virgil Trucks to Comiskey Park. Elliott hit .260 in 67 games with the Sox but Trucks won his first 8 decisions, had 13 complete games and a 15-6 record in 21 starts, finishing the year with a 20-10 overall record and a 2.93 ERA. Billy Pierce was 18-12 and his 2.72 was second-best in the league.

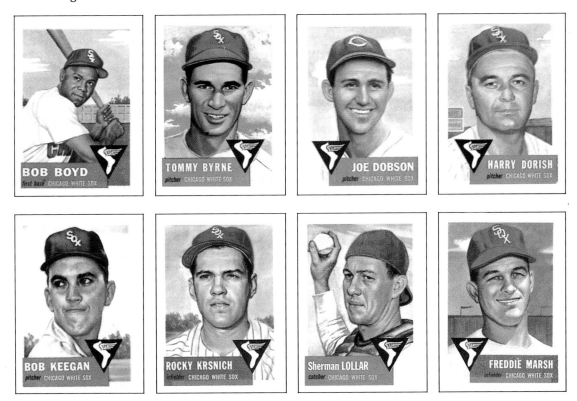

BOB BOYD
first base CHICAGO WHITE SOX

TOMMY BYRNE
pitcher CHICAGO WHITE SOX

JOE DOBSON
pitcher CHICAGO WHITE SOX

HARRY DORISH
pitcher CHICAGO WHITE SOX

BOB KEEGAN
pitcher CHICAGO WHITE SOX

ROCKY KRSNICH
infielder CHICAGO WHITE SOX

Sherman LOLLAR
catcher CHICAGO WHITE SOX

FREDDIE MARSH
infielder CHICAGO WHITE SOX

Orestes MINOSO — outfielder CHICAGO WHITE SOX

BILLY PIERCE — pitcher CHICAGO WHITE SOX

JIM RIVERA — outfielder CHICAGO WHITE SOX

Eddie ROBINSON — first base CHICAGO WHITE SOX

VERN STEPHENS — third base CHICAGO WHITE SOX

BOB WILSON — catcher CHICAGO WHITE SOX

1954

Although they finished third again, the Sox had an outstanding season with both Minnie Minoso and Nelson Fox in the batting race and four pitchers in the top 11 in the league ERA rankings. Minoso (.320) finished second in hitting and Fox (.319) third with Minoso also hitting 19 homers and driving in 116 runs. The final result was a 94-60 record, 17 games out. Paul Richards left to accept a general manager post in Baltimore and coach Marty Marion managed the team after Sept. 14.

Primarily responsible for the good showing were Virgil Trucks (19-12), Sandy Consuegra (16-3), Jack Harshman (14-8) and Bob Keegan (16-9). Consuegra led the league in winning percentage (.842) and was second in ERA (2.69) while Trucks, Harshman and Keegan all finished in the top 11. Injuries again sidelined Ferris Fain as well as third baseman George Kell and utilityman Cass Michaels who was beaned in Philadelphia, suffering a double skull fracture.

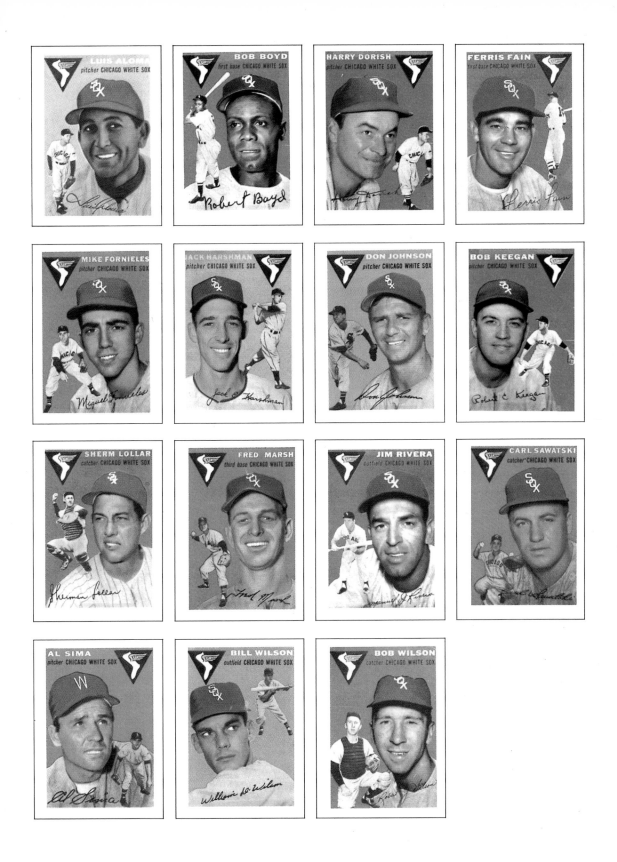

1955

Marty Marion's initial season as manager produced a 91-63 record that brought the White Sox closer (five games) to a first-place finish than any time in the previous 35 years but resulted in the fourth successive third-place finish. Minnie Minoso, key to the pennant chances, slumped during the first half of the season (hitting .254 with only 2 home runs at the All-Star break) but surged in the second half to finish at .288 with 10 homers and 70 RBIs.

George Kell's .312 average was third best in the league and Nellie Fox's .311 was fourth highest, contributing to a team batting average of .268 that led the league. Lefthander Billy Pierce (15-10) topped the league with his 1.97 ERA while Dick Donovan was 15-9, Virgil Trucks 13-8 and another southpaw, Jack Harshman, 11-7. Kell's 81 RBIs led the team. Walt Dropo had a team-high 19 homers and 79 RBIs.

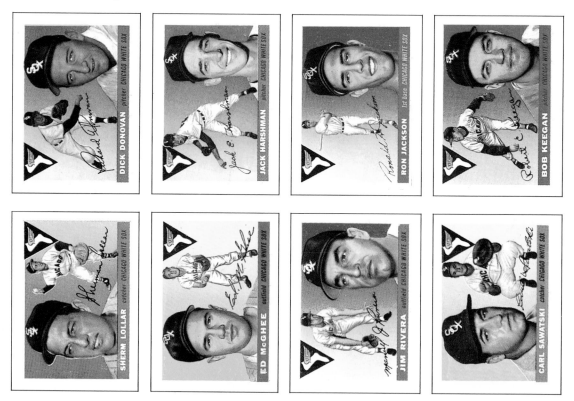

1956

Standing second for slightly over a month into mid-July and only four games out when an 11-game losing streak began on July 7, the White Sox slipped to fourth then rallied with 17 wins in 23 games to finish third for the fifth straight year (85-69). Lefty Billy Pierce started 14-4, won his 20th on Sept. 13 but finished 20-9. Jim Wilson, obtained from Baltimore in May in a six-player deal, began 11-4 through July 3 but lost his next eight decisions and wound up 13-14. Jack Harshman was 15-11. Minnie Minoso hit .316 with 21 homers and 88 RBIs while Larry Doby, acquired from Cleveland in the off-season for Jim Busby and Chico Carrasquel, batted .268 with club-high homer (24) and RBI (102) totals, helping set a club record of 128 homers.

Baseball's only woman club president, Mrs. Grace Comiskey, daughter-in-law of founder Charles A. Comiskey, died Dec. 10. Marty Marion was relieved as manager after the season and replaced by Al Lopez.

1957

Opening the season with 11 wins in 13 games, the White Sox started with a rush that saw them six games ahead of the field by June 8, but losing 14 of 22 to New York eventually helped the Sox settle to second (90-64), eight games behind the Yankees. Luis Aparicio, moved into shortstop after Chico Carrasquel was traded before the 1956 season, led a running game that produced 109 stolen bases. Aparicio stole 28 and Minnie Minoso and Jim Rivera 18 each. Nelson Fox hit .317, Minoso .310 (with 12 homers and 103 RBIs) while Larry Doby (.288) had 14 homers. For the second straight year, Billy Pierce (20-12) won 20 games. Dick Donovan was 16-6, Jim Wilson 15-8 and Bob Keegan 10-8. Keegan produced one of the highlights of the season on Aug. 8 when he pitched a no-hitter against Washington, winning 6-0 in the first such gem at Comiskey Park since 1940 and the first by a White Sox hurler anywhere since 1937.

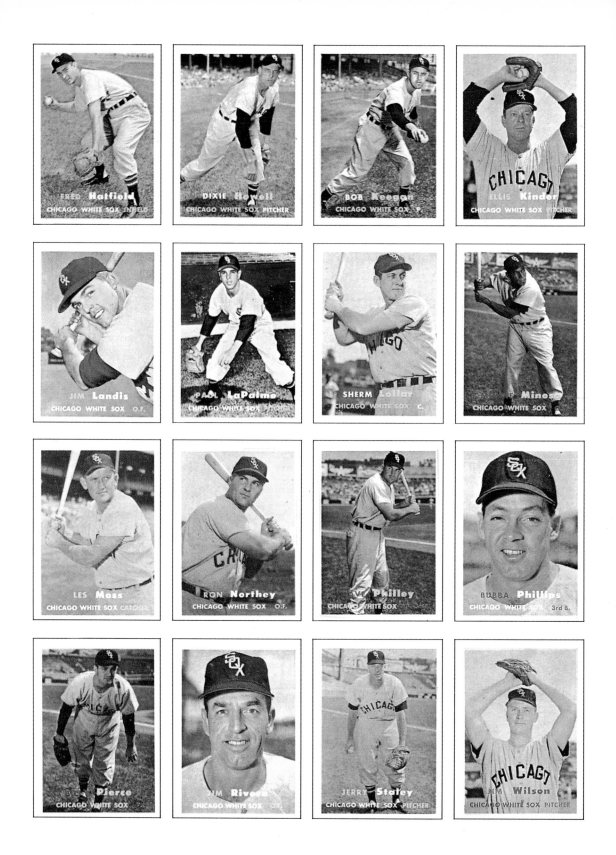

FRED **Hatfield**
CHICAGO WHITE SOX INFIELD

DIXIE **Howell**
CHICAGO WHITE SOX PITCHER

BOB **Keegan**
CHICAGO WHITE SOX P.

ELLIS **Kinder**
CHICAGO WHITE SOX PITCHER

JIM **Landis**
CHICAGO WHITE SOX O.F.

PAUL **LaPalme**
CHICAGO WHITE SOX

SHERM **Lollar**
CHICAGO WHITE SOX C.

Minoso
CHICAGO WHITE SOX

LES **Moss**
CHICAGO WHITE SOX CATCHER

RON **Northey**
CHICAGO WHITE SOX O.F.

Philley
CHICAGO WHITE SOX

BUBBA **Phillips**
CHICAGO WHITE SOX 3rd B.

Pierce
CHICAGO WHITE SOX

JIM **Rivera**
CHICAGO WHITE SOX O.F.

JERRY **Staley**
CHICAGO WHITE SOX PITCHER

JIM **Wilson**
CHICAGO WHITE SOX PITCHER

1958

A horrid start plunged the team into the cellar until mid-June and kept it under .500 until early August, but a strong finish brought the White Sox home second (82-72) for the second time in Al Lopez's two years as manager. While the club's 101 homers were low in the league its 101 stolen bases were more than double any other team (Cleveland had 50) with Luis Aparicio stealing 29, Jim Rivera 21 and Jim Landis 19 to finish one-two-three in the league. With Minoso traded to the Indians in the offseason for infielder Al Smith and pitcher Early Wynn, Nellie Fox's .300 was the team's top average. Landis hit .277, Aparicio .266 and catcher Sherm Lollar .273 with a club-high 20 homers and 84 RBIs. Billy Pierce (17-11) was second in the league with a 2.68 ERA and Dick Donovan (15-14) eighth with a 3.01 while Wynn was 14-16.

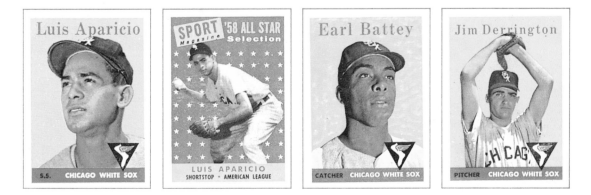

1959

On March 10, Bill Veeck along with Arthur Allyn and Hank Greenberg bought control of the White Sox from Mrs. Dorothy Comiskey Rigney, ending the family's control of the team that dated back to its founding in the 19th century in St. Paul, Minn.

Veeck's club promptly won its first pennant since 1919 with a 94-60 record that generated a five-game edge over second-place Cleveland. In the World Series the White Sox won game one (11-0 behind Early Wynn) and game five as Bob Shaw outpitched Sandy Koufax, 1-0, but the Los Angeles Dodgers won in six games. Most Valuable Player Nelson Fox hit .306 and Luis Aparicio .257 with 56 stolen bases, most in the league since 1943. Wynn was 22-10 but Bob Shaw was the surprise of the staff with an 18-6 record and a 2.69 ERA that was third best in the league. Billy Pierce was .14-15. Out of the bullpen, veteran Gerry Staley was 8-5 with a 2.25 ERA and Turk Lown 9-2 in 60 games.

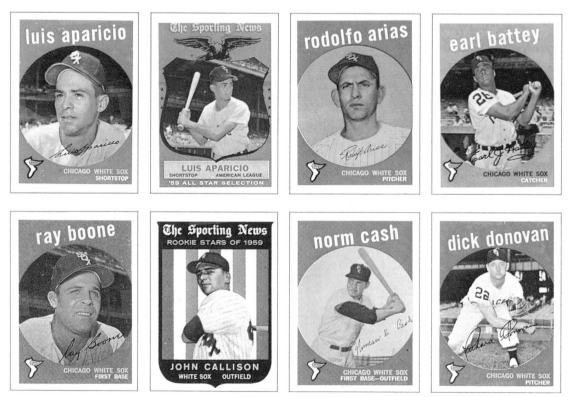

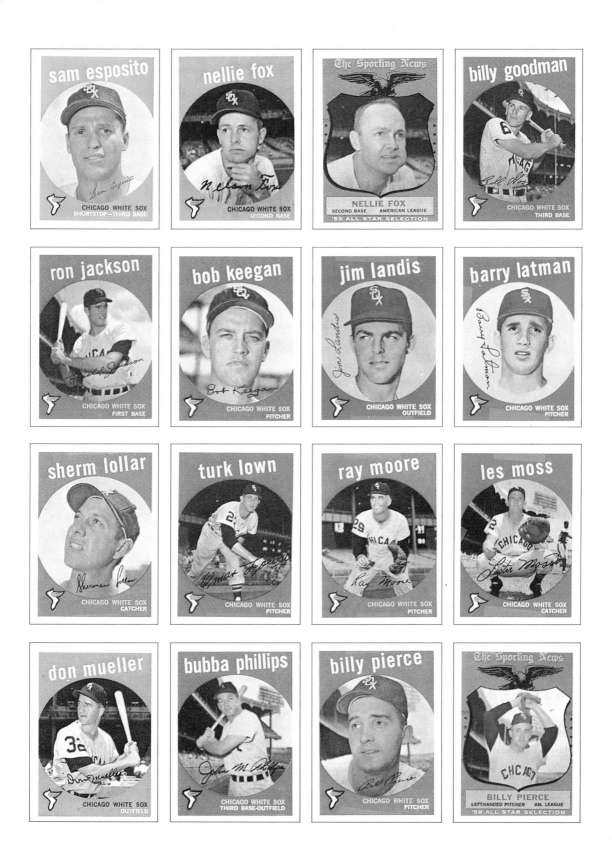

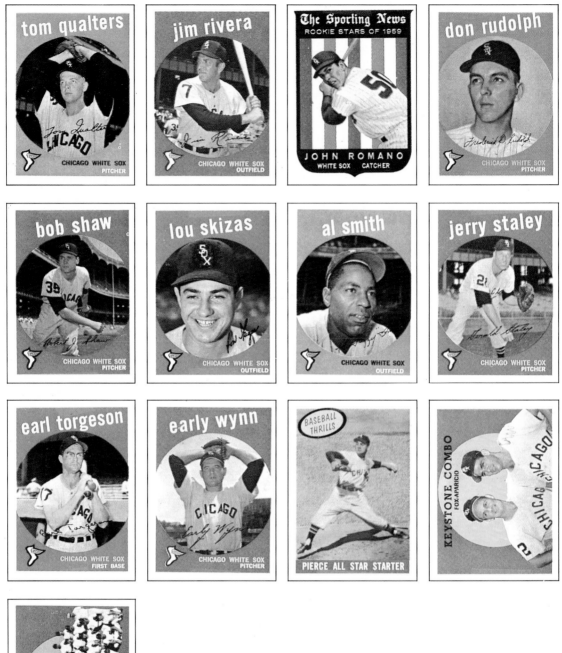

tom qualters
CHICAGO WHITE SOX
PITCHER

jim rivera
CHICAGO WHITE SOX
OUTFIELD

The Sporting News
ROOKIE STARS OF 1959
JOHN ROMANO
WHITE SOX   CATCHER

don rudolph
CHICAGO WHITE SOX
PITCHER

bob shaw
CHICAGO WHITE SOX
PITCHER

lou skizas
CHICAGO WHITE SOX
OUTFIELD

al smith
CHICAGO WHITE SOX
OUTFIELD

jerry staley
CHICAGO WHITE SOX
PITCHER

earl torgeson
CHICAGO WHITE SOX
FIRST BASE

early wynn
CHICAGO WHITE SOX
PITCHER

BASEBALL
THRILLS
PIERCE ALL STAR STARTER

KEYSTONE COMBO
FOX-APARICIO

CHICAGO
White Sox

While attendance soared to 1,644,460 (more than double the 797,451 of 1958) in the aftermath of the championship season, the team slumped to its almost traditional third-place spot with an 87-67 record, 10 games out of first. It was the first time in 14 years that Al Lopez managed a team finishing lower than second. Al Smith hit .315, the re-acquired Minnie Minoso .311, Roy Sievers .295 and Nelson Fox .289 as the team led the league with a .270 team average. Sievers had 28 homers and 93 RBIs while Minoso added 20 homers and 105 RBIs. Minoso also had 17 stolen bases, Jim Landis 23 and Luis Aparicio, who led the league for the fifth straight year, 51. Billy Pierce led the pitchers in wins (14-7) but Frank Baumann (13-6), one of the club's four 13-game winners, led the league with his 2.68 ERA. Other 13-game winners were Early Wynn (13-12), Bob Shaw (13-13) and reliever Gerry Staley (13-8) in 64 games.

1961

Another sluggish start led to a season of struggle as the White Sox were last as late as June 11 before ripping off 19 wins in 20 games (including 12 in a row) to move up to a final fourth-place finish (86-76), 23 games out. One of the few bright lights early in the year was veteran pitcher Early Wynn who was 8-2 but then quit for the season in July with shoulder problems. Juan Pizarro was the only pitcher to win more than 10 games, finishing 14-7 with a 3.05 ERA. Rookie outfielder Floyd Robinson led the club with a .310 average in 132 games with 11 homers and 59 RBIs. Roy Sievers hit .295 with 27 homers and 92 RBIs, Al Smith was .278 with 28 homers and 93 RBIs and Jim Landis hit .282 with 22 homers and 85 RBIs.

Luis Aparicio (.272) had 53 stolen bases in 66 attempts and once again led the league in steals. After a 7-6 April, the White Sox suffered a 9-21 May that doomed their pennant hopes.

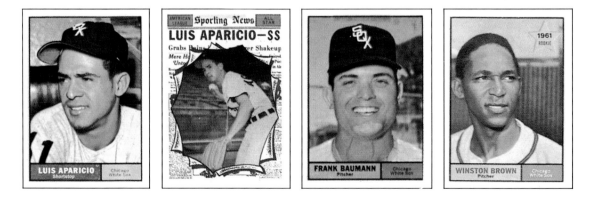

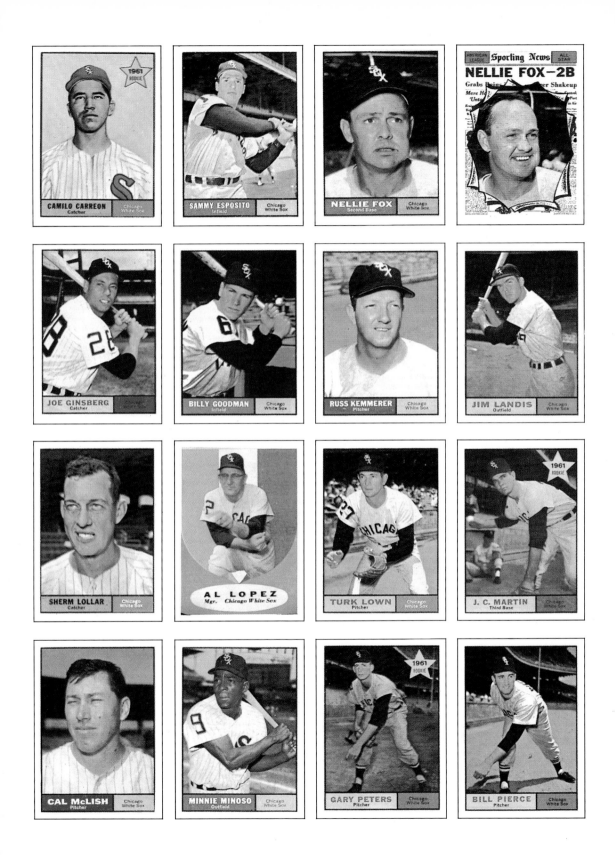

JUAN PIZARRO	JIM RIVERA	BOB ROSELLI	HERB SCORE
Pitcher	Outfield	Catcher	Pitcher
Chicago White Sox	Chicago White Sox	Chicago White Sox	Chicago White Sox

BOB SHAW	ROY SIEVERS	AL SMITH	JERRY STALEY
Pitcher	First Base	Outfield	Pitcher
Chicago White Sox	Chicago White Sox	Chicago White Sox	Chicago White Sox

EARL TORGESON	EARLY WYNN	AL'S ACES	CHICAGO WHITE SOX
First Base	Pitcher	Early Wynn • Al Lopez • Herb Score	
Chicago White Sox	Chicago White Sox		

1961 ROOKIE

1962

With the Allyn brothers, John and Arthur, now in full ownership of the club, the team on the field continued to skid. The record of 85-77 produced a fifth-place finish, the lowest for the White Sox since 1950 and the lowest of Al Lopez's managerial career in the major leagues. Floyd Robinson continued to be a star on the rise in his second season, leading the club in batting (.312) and RBIs (109), setting a team record for doubles (45) and adding home runs. Al Smith (.292) led the team with 16 homers (lowest total to lead the team since Minnie Minoso's 15 in 1953) and had 82 RBIs. Joe Cunningham hit .295 with 10 homers and 70 RBIs.

Luis Aparicio led the league in stolen bases for the seventh season in a row with 31 but he hit only .241 and the Sox stole only 76 bases as a team. In January 1963, Aparicio was traded to Baltimore for four players including reliever Hoyt Wilhelm. Ray Herbert (10-9) led the team in victories by winning his last six starts.

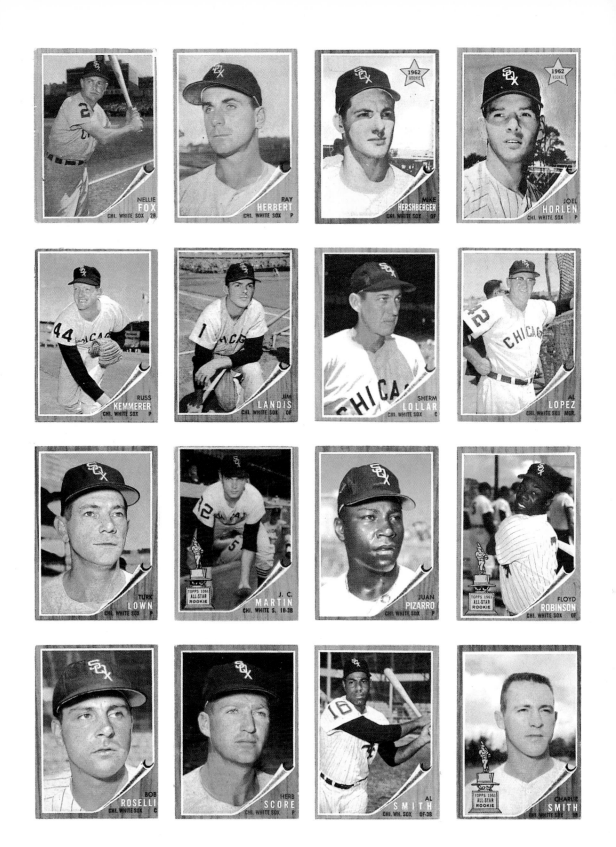

1963

Armed with the four players from Baltimore obtained in the trade for Luis Aparicio and a couple of young pitchers, the White Sox jumped up to second place with a 94-68 record although still 10½ games out. Pete Ward, one of the former Orioles, led the club in eight offensive departments including batting (.295), RBIs (84) and home runs (22), where he shared the leadership with free-swinging rookie Dave Nicholson who struck out a then-record 175 times and hit .229 but drove in 70 runs. But it was the pitching that was primarily responsible for the upward move. The club led the league with 21 shutouts and a 2.97 team ERA. Gary Peters was 19-8, leading the league with a 2.33 ERA and Juan Pizarro was 16-8 with a 2.39 ERA that was second-best in the league despite arm and shoulder problems. From July 11, Peters won 11 straight decisions including 10 complete games in a row. Ray Herbert was 8-4 on June 17 but suffered a groin pull and finished 13-10.

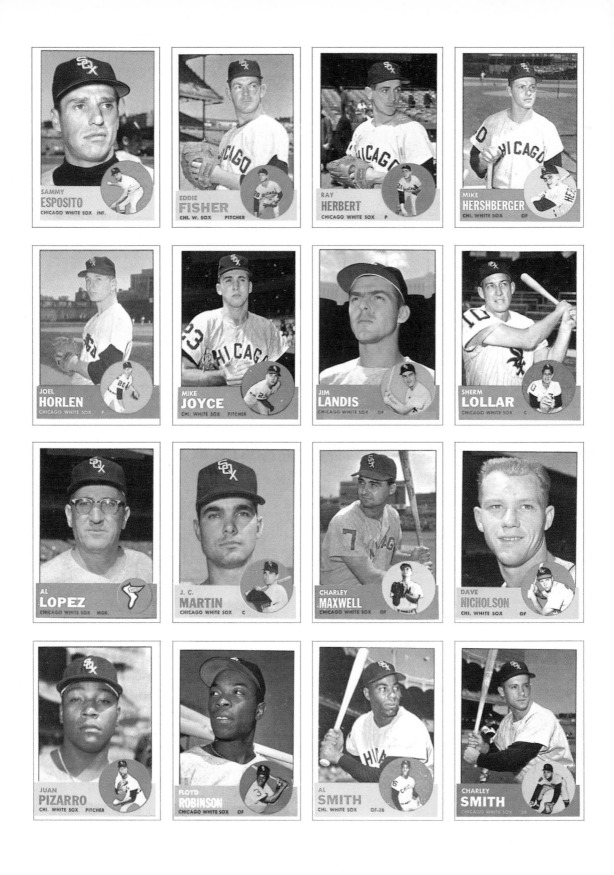

SAMMY
ESPOSITO
CHICAGO WHITE SOX INF.

EDDIE
FISHER
CHI. W. SOX PITCHER

RAY
HERBERT
CHICAGO WHITE SOX P

MIKE
HERSHBERGER
CHI. WHITE SOX OF

JOEL
HORLEN
CHICAGO WHITE SOX P

MIKE
JOYCE
CHI. WHITE SOX PITCHER

JIM
LANDIS
CHICAGO WHITE SOX OF

SHERM
LOLLAR
CHICAGO WHITE SOX C

AL
LOPEZ
CHICAGO WHITE SOX MGR.

J. C.
MARTIN
CHICAGO WHITE SOX C

CHARLEY
MAXWELL
CHICAGO WHITE SOX OF

DAVE
NICHOLSON
CHI. WHITE SOX OF

JUAN
PIZARRO
CHI. WHITE SOX PITCHER

FLOYD
ROBINSON
CHICAGO WHITE SOX OF

AL
SMITH
CHI. WHITE SOX OF-3B

CHARLEY
SMITH
CHICAGO WHITE SOX 3B

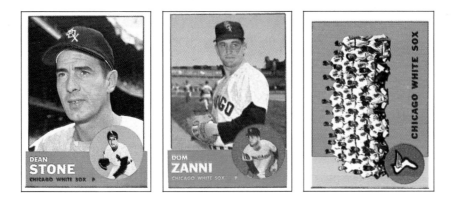

1964

Here, even more than five years earlier, was a race for the pennant, a real race. Unfortunately the White Sox lost it to the Yankees by a single game and Al Lopez, the only manager to win an American League pennant over the Yankees since 1948, was unable to add a third flag to his collection.

Trailing by six games June 23, the Sox won 18 of 23 and moved into first, remained tied for the lead as late as Sept. 16 but were eliminated on the next-to-last day of the season with a 98-64 record, the most wins for the team since 1917. Losing the first 10 meetings to the Yankees hurt but not as much as Ray Herbert's elbow injury that held his record to 6-7. Gary Peters was 20-8, Juan Pizarro 19-9 and Joel Horlen 13-9. Pete Ward hit .282 with a club-high 23 homers and 94 RBIs while Floyd Robinson had a team-best .301 average. Shortstop Ron Hansen hit .261 but hammered 20 homers with 68 RBIs.

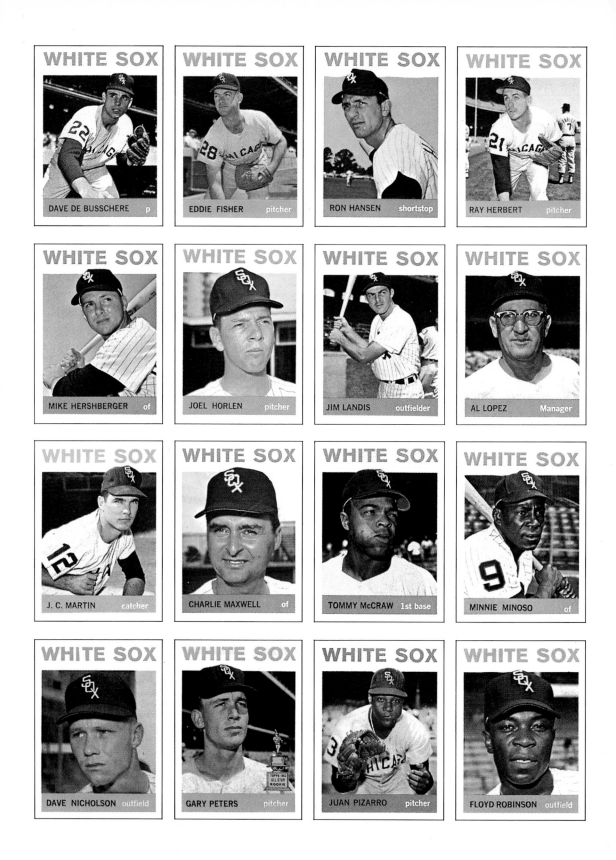

WHITE SOX
GENE STEPHENS   outfield

WHITE SOX
PETE WARD   3rd base

WHITE SOX
AL WEIS   2b-ss

WHITE SOX
HOYT WILHELM   pitcher

1964 ROOKIE STARS
WHITE SOX
FRITZ ACKLEY   PITCHER
DON BUFORD   2B-3B

1964 ROOKIE STARS
WHITE SOX
BRUCE HOWARD   PITCHER
FRANK KREUTZER   PITCHER

CHICAGO WHITE SOX

1965

Fourth at the All-Star break, the White Sox went on a 10-game winning streak in August that boosted them to second, and they closed to within 4 ½ games of league-leading Minnesota in September but then lost five straight to fall out of the race, finishing 95-67, in second place, seven games out. Reliever Eddie Fisher set a league record with 82 game appearances and was 15-7 with a 2.40 ERA. Among the starters, lefthander Tommy John was 14-7, John Buzhardt was 13-8, Joel Horlen was 13-13 despite a 2.88 ERA and Gary Peters slumped to 10-12. Don Buford was the leading hitter with a .283 average and former Yankee Bill Skowron hit .274 with a club-high 18 homers and 78 RBIs. Catcher John Romano also hit 18 while Pete Ward fell to .247. After nine years at the helm Al Lopez stepped down at the end of the season and was succeeded by Eddie Stanky. Lopez, who returned briefly two years later, was an impressive 811-615 over the nine seasons.

1966

After a 10-3 start for new manager Eddie Stanky, the White Sox were victimized by a porous defense that committed 46 errors in the first 36 games, and a spring-training injury to reliever Hoyt Wilhelm that kept him out of action until June 14. Eventually, the team finished fourth (83-79).

Rookie Tommie Agee led the hitters with a .273 mark as the Sox had a .231 team average, lowest for the team since 1910 and the lowest in the league with only 87 homers, second-lowest in the league. Agee had 22 homers and 86 RBIs as well as 44 stolen bases; Ken Berry hit .271. Ron Hansen underwent surgery on June 3 for a ruptured spinal disc and Pete Ward on May 29 for a hernia. Gary Peters (12-10) was also hurt and missed two weeks. Tommy John was 14-11, Joel Horlen 10-13 with a 2.43 ERA and Bruce Howard 9-5 with a 2.30 ERA as the team compiled a 2.68 ERA and led the majors with 22 shutouts.

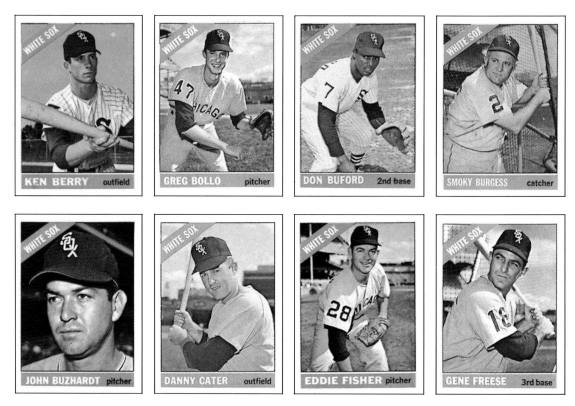

KEN BERRY   outfield   GREG BOLLO   pitcher   DON BUFORD   2nd base   SMOKY BURGESS   catcher

JOHN BUZHARDT   pitcher   DANNY CATER   outfield   EDDIE FISHER   pitcher   GENE FREESE   3rd base

 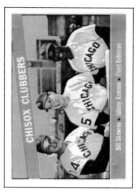  

1967

Powered by an awesome pitching performance, the White Sox held first place for 89 days including 62 in a row into mid-August before finally winding up fourth (89-73) only three games behind in a wild four-team scramble. Tied for first as late as Sept. 6, the Sox lost their final five games to negate a team ERA of 2.16, lowest in the league since 1917. Three of the first four pitchers ranked in ERA in the league were Joel Horlen (19-7), first at 2.06, Gary Peters (16-11), second at 2.28 and Tommy John (10-13), fourth at 2.48. Horlen pitched a no-hitter against Detroit, winning 6-0 on Sept. 10 at Comiskey Park and also a 2-hitter, three 3-hitters and six shutouts. In the bullpen, Hoyt Wilhelm was 8-3 with a 1.31 ERA, Bob Locker 7-5 (2.09) in 77 games and Don McMahon 6-2 (1.98). Hitting produced the lowest team average (.225) in the league for a first-division team since 1909 with Ken Berry and Don Buford at .241.

≡1968≡

A rash of injuries crippled the pitching staff and with them went the pennant hopes for a team that finished eighth with a 67-95 record, 36 games out of the lead. Eddie Stanky was fired as manager July 12 with the team 35-45 and ninth. Al Lopez returned but coach Les Moss took over when Lopez had an appendectomy on Aug. 23 and missed a month. Moss was 12-24.

Even the return of Luis Aparicio didn't help the team which produced a meager 463 runs with Tommy Davis hitting .268, Aparicio .264 and Ken Berry .252. Pete Ward led the team with only 15 homers. Gary Peters (4-13) had a groin pull, Joel Horlen (12-14) shoulder problems, and Tommy John (10-5) tore a shoulder ligament in a fight and missed six weeks. Bullpen ace Wilbur Wood (13-12) set a league record of 88 games and Hoyt Wilhelm (4-4) was in 72. Nine "home" games played in Milwaukee drew 265,452, allowing the White Sox to total 803,775 for the season.

| SANDY ALOMAR | LUIS APARICIO | KEN BERRY | KEN BOYER |
| WAYNE CAUSEY | ROCKY COLAVITO | TOMMY DAVIS | JACK FISHER |

JOE
HORLEN
PITCHER · WHITE SOX

JOE HORLEN
PITCHER · AMERICAN LEAGUE
The Sporting News
68
ALL STAR SELECTION
★ ★ ★

TOMMY
JOHN
PITCHER · WHITE SOX

DUANE
JOSEPHSON
CATCHER · WHITE SOX

FRED
KLAGES
PITCHER · WHITE SOX

BOB
LOCKER
PITCHER · WHITE SOX

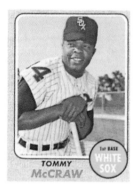

TOMMY
McCRAW
1st BASE · WHITE SOX

DON
McMAHON
PITCHER · WHITE SOX

JERRY
McNERTNEY
CATCHER · WHITE SOX

GARY
PETERS
PITCHER · WHITE SOX

GARY PETERS
PITCHER · AMERICAN LEAGUE
The Sporting News
68
ALL STAR SELECTION
★ ★ ★

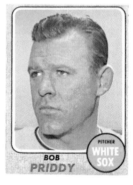

BOB
PRIDDY
PITCHER · WHITE SOX

RUSS
SNYDER
OUTFIELD · WHITE SOX

EDDIE
STANKY
MANAGER · WHITE SOX

PETE
WARD
3B-1B · WHITE SOX

HOYT
WILHELM
PITCHER · WHITE SOX

1969

Al Lopez started his final major league managerial season but resigned on May 3 with the team 8-9, and coach Don Gutteridge finished a season that produced a 68-94 record and a fifth-place finish (in the new West division), 29 games out. Comiskey Park's dimensions were reduced from 352 feet down the foul lines to 335 feet and from 415 feet to 400 feet in center, but only 29 more home runs were hit (15 by the Sox). Walt Williams hit .304 to lead the hitters while Bill Melton (.255) had 23 homers and 87 RBIs. Luis Aparicio hit .280. Joel Horlen (13-16) was the top-winning starter while Wilbur Wood had 15 saves and 10-11 record in 76 relief games. Attendance for 70 games was 392,862, bolstered by another 196,684 in 11 games at Milwaukee for a total of 589,546. On Sept. 25 Arthur Allyn sold his 50 percent interest to his brother John, making him sole owner of the team.

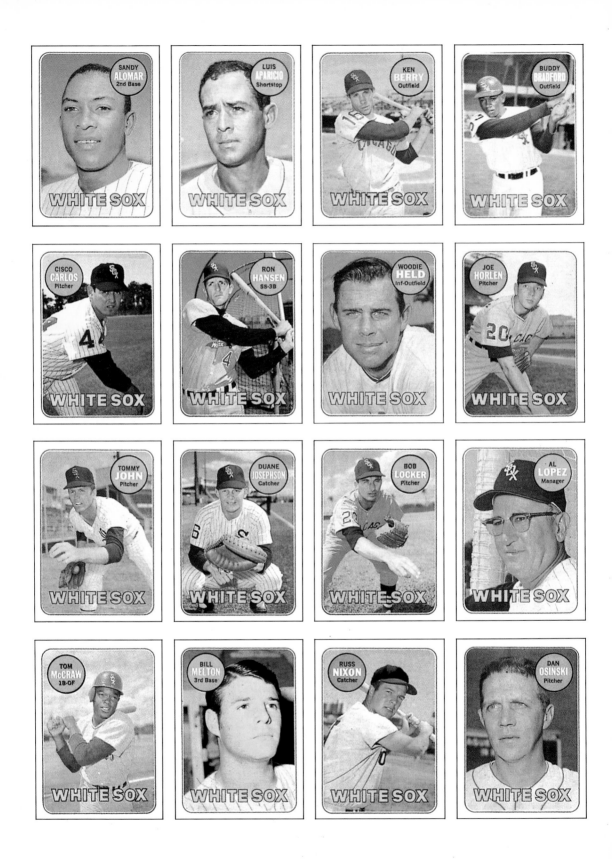

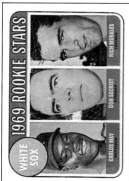

1970

Perhaps the worst season in White Sox history. The club was 56-106, the most losses ever, with Don Gutteridge fired on Sept. 3 in a front-office shakeup. He was replaced by Chuck Tanner. Aparicio was one of the few bright spots, hitting .313 (fourth best in the league) and breaking Luke Appling's record of 2,219 games at shortstop. With Gary Peters traded to Boston, Joel Horlen (6-16) and Tommy John (12-17) struggled despite help from Jerry Janeski (10-17) and reliever Wilbur Wood (9-13) with 21 saves.

Off the field, the arrival of the Brewers in Milwaukee cut off an avenue of attendance. With all games in Comiskey Park the gate fell to 495,355, the lowest for the team since 1942. Carlos May made a remarkable comeback from a freak accident during a tour of Marine reserve duty in 1969, partially destroying his hand. May batted .285 with 12 homers and 68 RBIs.

Luis Aparicio | SHORTSTOP

Gerry Arrigo | PITCHER

Ken Berry | OUTFIELD

Buddy Bradford | OUTFIELD

Bob Christian | OUTFIELD

Paul Edmondson | PITCHER

Don Gutteridge | MANAGER

Ron Hansen | 2B-SHORTSTOP

WHITE SOX Ed Herrmann — CATCHER	**WHITE SOX** Gail Hopkins — 1ST BASE	**WHITE SOX** Joe Horlen — PITCHER	**WHITE SOX** Tommy John — PITCHER
WHITE SOX Duane Josephson — CATCHER	**WHITE SOX** Bobby Knoop — 2ND BASE	**WHITE SOX** Carlos May — OUTFIELD	**WHITE SOX** Tom McCraw — 1ST BASE
WHITE SOX Bill Melton — 3RD BASE	**WHITE SOX** Rich Morales — 2B-3B	**WHITE SOX** Danny Murphy — PITCHER	**WHITE SOX** Walt Williams — OUTFIELD
WHITE SOX Wilbur Wood — PITCHER	**WHITE SOX** Billy Wynne — PITCHER	**1970 ROOKIE STARS WHITE SOX** BILLY FARMER — PITCHER JOHN MATIAS — 1B-OF	**1970 ROOKIE STARS WHITE SOX** MICKEY SCOTT — PITCHER DAN LAZAR — PITCHER BART JOHNSON — PITCHER

≡1971

After a dismal sixth-place finish in the West, 42 games behind, nine deals involving 31 players were made by new general manager Stu Holcomb and player-personnel chief Roland Hemond with only seven players returning from the previous season. After an opening-day win before a record 43,253, the White Sox lost the next seven and dropped into the cellar. But the team struggled back to finish third (79-83), 22½ games back.

Bill Melton, shifted to third base from the outfield, became the first White Sox home run champion (33) with 86 RBIs and a .269 average. Carlos May continued his comeback with a .294 season. Wilbur Wood, switched to a starting role, worked 334 innings (most for a White Sox since 1922), and finishing 22-13 with 22 complete games was second in the league with a 1.91 ERA. Tom Bradley was 15-15 with a 2.96 ERA and Tommy John 13-16 while new relief ace Bart Johnson (12-10) had 14 saves.

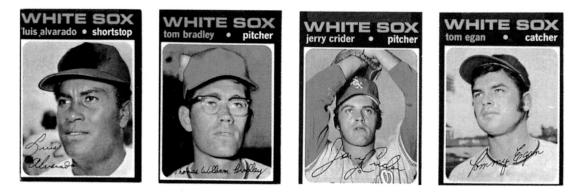

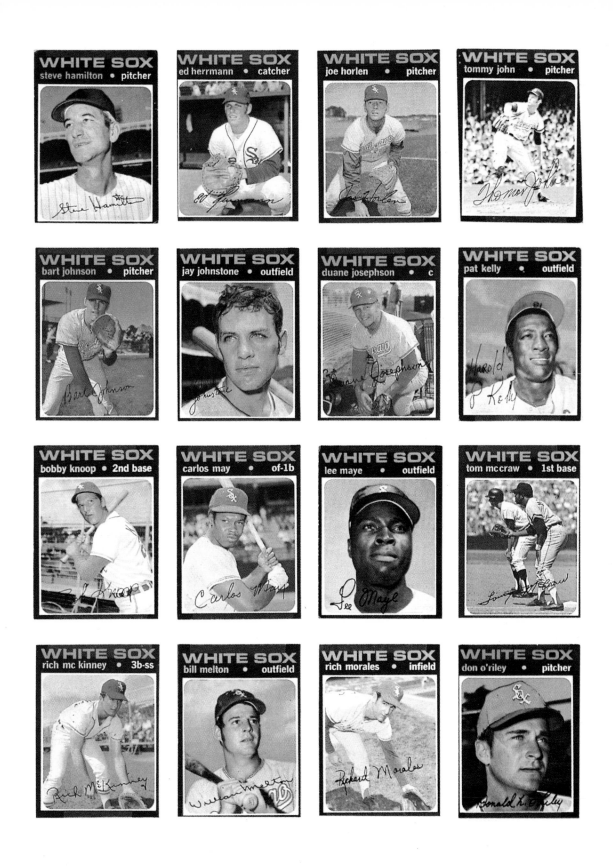

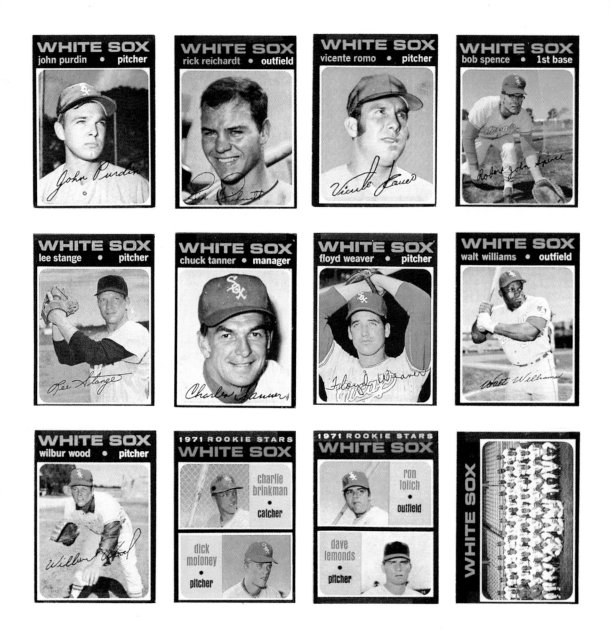

1972

A trade that brought temperamental but talented Richie (Dick) Allen from the Dodgers for lefthander Tommy John was the key to a major improvement in the offense that helped the Sox advance to second in the West (87-67), 5½ games out. Allen hammered a club-record 37 homers to lead the league and also was the league leader in RBIs (113) while hitting .308. Carlos May also hit .308 with 12 homers and 68 RBIs. Wilbur Wood continued his amazing pitching with a 24-17 record, a 2.51 ERA and 49 games started, matching a club record set by Ed Walsh in 1908. Wood and his two other starting mates, Stan Bahnsen (21-16) and Tom Bradley (15-14) started 130 of the 154 games played by the club. New relief ace Terry Forster (6-5) set a club record of 29 saves. For having the club in first place as late as Aug. 12, Chuck Tanner was named Manager of the Year and personnel director Roland Hemond picked as Executive of the Year.

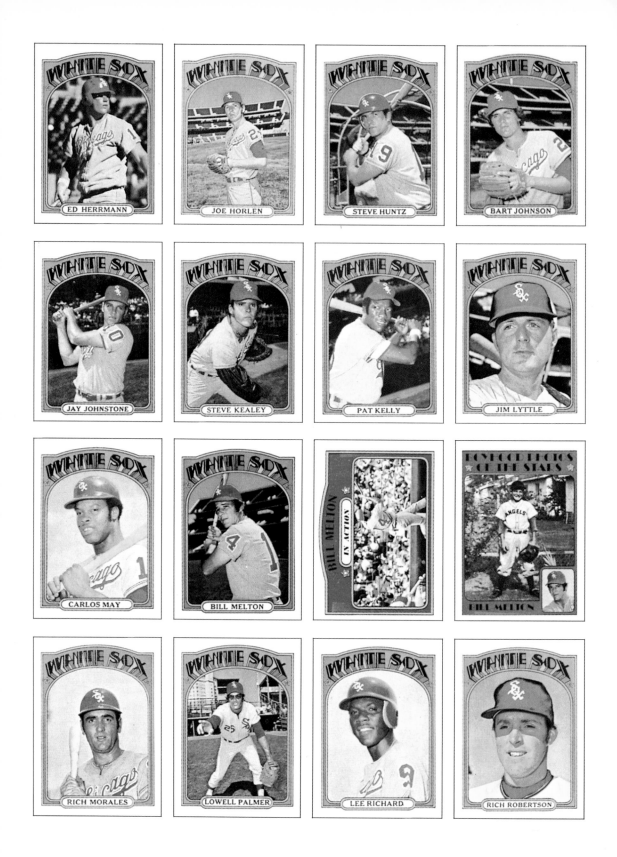

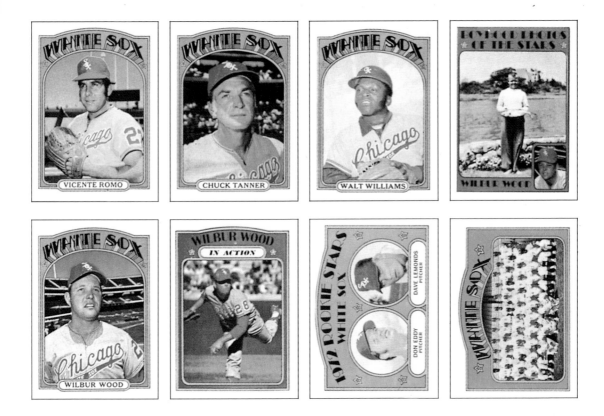

1973

A year of turmoil and disappointment for the White Sox came as the team was in first place regularly up to June 29 (58 days all told) but collapsed badly in the wake of an injury to Dick Allen and shallow starting pitching. Allen, the league's Most Valuable Player in 1972, hurt his ankle on June 28 and virtually disappeared thereafter, batting only five more times. Allen hit .316 in his 250 at-bats with 16 homers and 41 RBIs.

Carlos May (.268) had 20 homers and a club-high 96 RBIs while Bill Melton (.277) also had 20 homers and batted in 87 runs. Two players (Rick Reichardt and Mike Andrews) were unable to agree on contracts and were released during the season. Wilbur Wood (24-20) and Stan Bahnsen (18-21) combined for a staggering 90 starts, 48 for Wood, but the next-best pitcher was part-time starter Terry Forster (6-11) who led the club with a 3.23. General Manager Stu Holcomb resigned on July 27, leaving Roland Hemond in charge.

DAVE
LEMONDS
CHICAGO WHITE SOX
PITCHER

EDDIE
LEON
CHICAGO WHITE SOX
2nd BASE

CARLOS
MAY
CHICAGO WHITE SOX
OUTFIELD

BILL
MELTON
CHICAGO WHITE SOX
3rd BASE

RICH
MORALES
CHICAGO WHITE SOX
SHORTSTOP

TONY
MUSER
CHICAGO WHITE SOX
1st BASE

JORGE
ORTA
CHICAGO WHITE SOX
2nd BASE

COACHES
JOE LONNETT
AL MONCHAK
JIM MAHONEY
JOHNNY SAIN

CHUCK
TANNER
CHICAGO WHITE SOX
MANAGER

WILBUR
WOOD
CHICAGO WHITE SOX
PITCHER

CHICAGO WHITE SOX

1974

Dick Allen once again made the White Sox a factor in the West race, hitting .301 with 32 home runs and 88 RBIs in 128 games but then, on Sept. 13, when it seemed the team was out of the race, he announced he was "retiring from baseball." Although Allen eventually wound up playing for the Phillies the following season, his departure helped the Sox slide home 80-80 in fourth place, nine games out of first. Jorge Orta played a complete season, hitting .316 (second best in the league) and Ken Henderson (.292) hit 20 homers with 95 RBIs. Bill Melton struggled much of the year but finished at .240 with 21 homers and 63 RBIs.

Veteran lefty Jim Kaat, obtained from Minnesota, led the pitchers with a 21-13 record and 2.92 ERA; Wilbur Wood was 20-19 with a 3.60 ERA in 42 starts and young Bart Johnson, who also quit at the start of the season, returned to compile a 10-4 record and a 2.73 ERA in the second half.

1975

In perhaps the worst season of Chuck Tanner's five years as manager, the team staggered most of the year and finally finished 75-86, fifth in the West, 22½ games behind. Jorge Orta was the most consistent performer, batting .304 with 11 homers and 83 RBIs. Deron Johnson, released by Boston, was signed in spring training and provided some power with 19 homers and 75 RBIs despite a .239 average as Bill Melton slumped to .240 with only 15 homers and 70 RBIs. Johnson was sold back to Boston in September. Stan Bahnsen left even sooner, being traded to Oakland after a 4-6 start. Jim Kaat was 20-14 in 41 starts and Wilbur Wood 16-20 in 43. Rich Gossage (9-8) had a 1.84 ERA and 26 saves in 62 games. On Dec. 16 John Allyn, who lost some $2.5 million in 1975, sold 80 percent of the team to former owner Bill Veeck, who fired Tanner the next day and made six trades in two days after the sale.

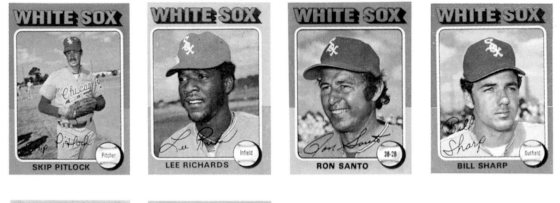

SKIP PITLOCK   LEE RICHARDS   RON SANTO   BILL SHARP

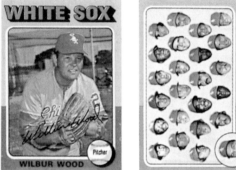

WILBUR WOOD

1976

New owner Bill Veeck brought in Paul Richards for a second tour as manager, ripped out the artificial turf (installed in 1968) in the infield and replaced it with grass and then tore down the fence in centerfield, increasing the home run distance from 415 feet to 440. Amid all these changes the White Sox had a terrible season on the field, posting the worst record both home and away in the league, finishing sixth, 64-97, 25½ games out. On May 9, Wilbur Wood, who had a 4-3 record, was hit by a line drive and suffered a fractured kneecap. He was lost for the season and things went downhill rapidly from there. Ken Brett (10-12) was the top winner among the remaining pitchers as Bart Johnson finished 9-16 and Rich Gossage 9-17. Ralph Garr topped the hitters, batting .300 in 136 games; Jim Spencer (.253) and Jorge Orta (.274) hit 14 home runs each and Orta had 72 RBIs.

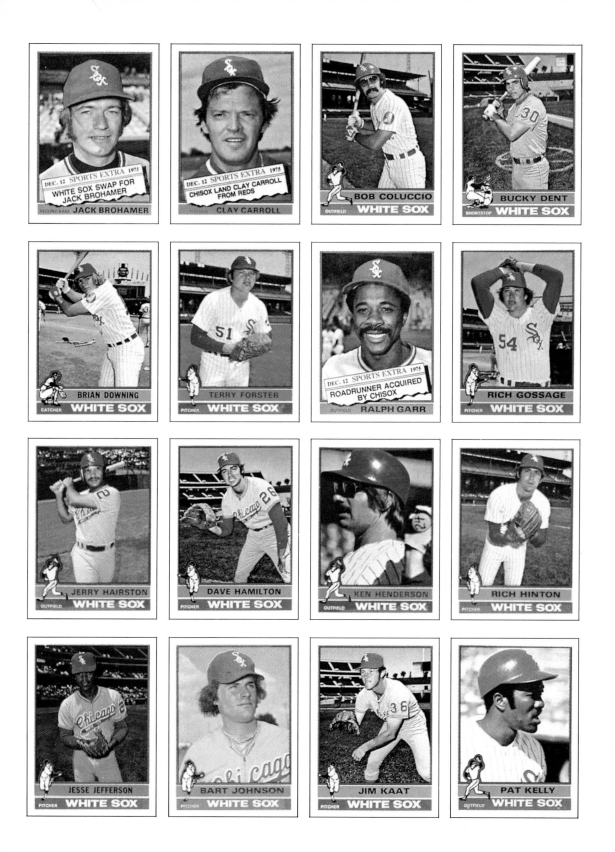

DEC. 12 SPORTS EXTRA 1975
WHITE SOX SWAP FOR
JACK BROHAMER
SECOND BASE **JACK BROHAMER**

DEC. 12 SPORTS EXTRA 1975
CHISOX LAND CLAY CARROLL
FROM REDS
PITCHER **CLAY CARROLL**

OUTFIELD **BOB COLUCCIO**

SHORTSTOP **BUCKY DENT**

CATCHER **WHITE SOX** BRIAN DOWNING

PITCHER **WHITE SOX** TERRY FORSTER

DEC. 12 SPORTS EXTRA 1975
ROADRUNNER ACQUIRED
BY CHISOX
OUTFIELD **RALPH GARR**

PITCHER **WHITE SOX** RICH GOSSAGE

OUTFIELD **WHITE SOX** JERRY HAIRSTON

PITCHER **WHITE SOX** DAVE HAMILTON

OUTFIELD **WHITE SOX** KEN HENDERSON

PITCHER **WHITE SOX** RICH HINTON

PITCHER **WHITE SOX** JESSE JEFFERSON

PITCHER **WHITE SOX** BART JOHNSON

PITCHER **WHITE SOX** JIM KAAT

OUTFIELD **WHITE SOX** PAT KELLY

CARLOS MAY
OUTFIELD **WHITE SOX**

BILL MELTON
THIRD BASE **WHITE SOX**

DEC. 11 SPORTS EXTRA 1975
WHITE SOX GET NETTLES
FROM ANGELS
OUTFIELD MORRIS NETTLES

NYLS NYMAN
OUTFIELD **WHITE SOX**

JORGE ORTA
SECOND BASE **WHITE SOX**

DAN OSBORN
PITCHER **WHITE SOX**

CLAUDE OSTEEN
PITCHER **WHITE SOX**

LEE RICHARD
SHORTSTOP **WHITE SOX**

DEC. 11 SPORTS EXTRA 1975
SPENCER TO CHISOX IN
4-PLAYER SWAP
FIRST BASE JIM SPENCER

BILL STEIN
THIRD BASE **WHITE SOX**

PETE VARNEY
CATCHER **WHITE SOX**

WILBUR WOOD
PITCHER **WHITE SOX**

MGR.
CHUCK TANNER
CHICAGO WHITE SOX

1977

With Paul Richards gone after one bad season, Bob Lemon became the manager and he wasn't the only new face. Bill Veeck, acting as his own general manager, rounded up a collection of free agents and castoffs to bolster the team and they combined to produce one of the most exciting seasons in several years.

Powered by a club record 192 home runs (second highest in the league), the Sox moved to third (90-72), 12 games out. Oscar Gamble hit .297 and socked 31 homers (most ever for a lefthanded hitter for the Sox) with 83 RBIs; Richie Zisk (.290) had 30 homers and 101 RBIs while Jim Spencer (.247) hit 18 as did Lamar Johnson (.302). Eric Soderholm, who missed the entire 1976 season through injury, was Comeback Player of the Year with 25 homers, 67 RBIs and a .280 average. Ralph Garr hit .300 again. Steve Stone (15-12), Francisco Barrios (14-7), Chris Knapp (12-7) and Ken Kravec (11-8) were the top pitchers as Wilbur Wood (7-8) struggled back from injury.

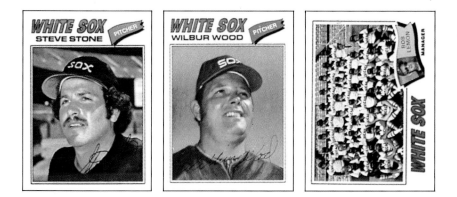

≡1978≡

After the excitement of the longball festival the year before, Oscar Gamble and Richie Zisk were among the missing, having opted for extravagant free-agent deals (as did infielder Jack Brohamer). Shortly, manager Bob Lemon was also gone. On June 30 Lemon was fired with the club 34-40 and 5½ games out. Larry Doby was named the manager but did no better, the White Sox finishing fifth (71-90), 20½ games behind. One of the name players acquired in the offseason shuffling was Bobby Bonds but he was traded to Texas for Claudell Washington on May 16. Washington, hitting .167 at Texas, batted .264 in 86 games at Chicago. Chet Lemon hit .300 with 13 homers and 55 RBIs and Wayne Nordhagen batted .301 although both battled injury all season. Jorge Orta (.274) also had 13 homers. Steve Stone (12-12), Ken Kravec (11-16) and Wilbur Wood (10-10) were the top winners and Lerrin LaGrow, who had 25 saves in 1976, saved 16.

ALAN BANNISTER

FRANCISCO BARRIOS

KEVIN BELL

RON BLOMBERG

WAYNE NORDHAGEN

JORGE ORTA

STEVE RENKO

RON SCHUELER

ERIC SODERHOLM

JIM SPENCER

ROYLE STILLMAN

STEVE STONE

JOHN VERHOEVEN

WILBUR WOOD

1979

Don Kessinger, one-time hero for the crosstown Cubs, became the playing manager but lasted only till Aug. 2 as the White Sox staggered into fifth place. Tony LaRussa took over when Kessinger retired on Aug. 2 and was 27-27 as the team finished fifth, 73-87, 14 games behind. July 12 was a depressing night as an anti-Disco promotion turned into a near-riot and the Sox had to forfeit the second game of a twi-night doubleheader to the Detroit Tigers. Chet Lemon continued his fine all-around play with a .318 average, 17 homers and 86 RBIs. Lemon's average was the best for a Sox hitter since Minnie Minoso's .320 in 1954. Lamar Johnson (.309) had 12 homers and 74 RBIs but Jim Morrison, obtained from the Phillies on July 10, hit .275 with 14 homers and 35 RBIs in just 67 games. Eric Soderholm was traded to Texas for Ed Farmer who had 14 saves in 44 games for the Sox. Ken Kravec (15-13), Ross Baumgarten (13-8) and Rich Wortham (14-14) were the top winners.

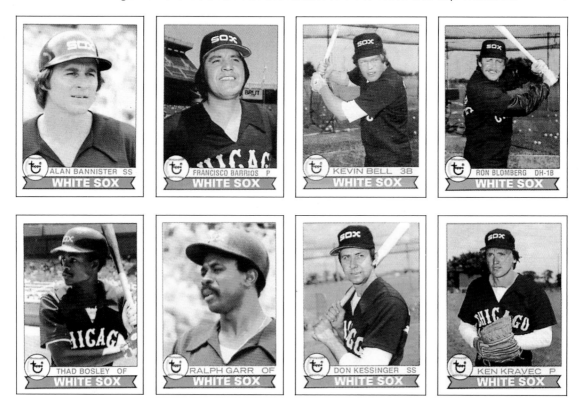

ALAN BANNISTER SS — WHITE SOX

FRANCISCO BARRIOS P — WHITE SOX

KEVIN BELL 3B — WHITE SOX

RON BLOMBERG DH-1B — WHITE SOX

THAD BOSLEY OF — WHITE SOX

RALPH GARR OF — WHITE SOX

DON KESSINGER SS — WHITE SOX

KEN KRAVEC P — WHITE SOX

LERRIN LaGROW P — WHITE SOX
CHET LEMON OF — WHITE SOX
BOB MOLINARO OF — WHITE SOX
JUNIOR MOORE 3B-2B — WHITE SOX

BILL NAHORODNY C — WHITE SOX
WAYNE NORDHAGEN OF-C — WHITE SOX
JORGE ORTA 2B — WHITE SOX
MIKE PROLY P — WHITE SOX

GREG PRYOR 3B-SS — WHITE SOX
RON SCHUELER P — WHITE SOX
ERIC SODERHOLM 3B — WHITE SOX
STEVE STONE P — WHITE SOX

PABLO TORREALBA P — WHITE SOX
CLAUDELL WASHINGTON OF — WHITE SOX
JIM WILLOUGHBY P — WHITE SOX
WILBUR WOOD P — WHITE SOX

≡1980≡

On Jan. 19, Bill Veeck's second and final tour as owner of the White Sox ended with the sale of the club to real estate developer Jerry Reinsdorf and television executive Eddie Einhorn.

In first place on May 23 with a 22-16 record, the Sox lost three straight in Seattle and began a downward slide that finally placed them fifth, 70-90, 26 games out. Chet Lemon (.292) was the top hitter and Lamar Johnson (.277) had 13 homers and 81 RBIs but no other hitter had more than 59 RBIs. Jim Morrison (.283) and Wayne Nordhagen (.277) had 15 homers apiece. Three rookies starred for the pitchers. Britt Burns (15-13) had a 2.84 ERA (third best in the league), Rich Dotson was 12-10 and LaMarr Hoyt was 9-3 despite not making his first start until July. Out of the bullpen, Ed Farmer (7-9) set a club record with 30 saves and Mike Proly (5-10) had 8.

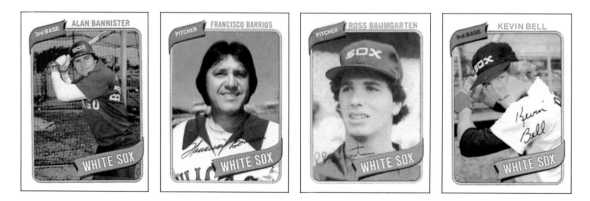

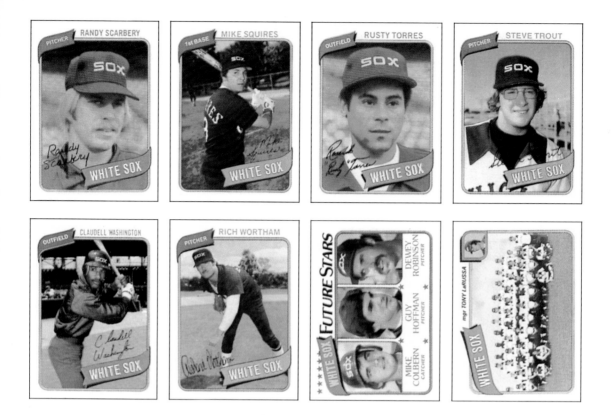

1981

A good start (winning 11 of the first 15) was wasted when the players' strike began with the White Sox third (31-22), only 2½ games out in the West. In the second half, a 23-30 record was good for no better than sixth (54-52 overall). But the character of the team changed with the acquisition of free-agent catcher Carlton Fisk and the trade for slugger Greg Luzinski from the Phillies. Fisk hit .263 in the shortened season with 45 RBIs and Luzinski (.265) clubbed 21 homers with 62 RBIs. Chet Lemon led the team with a .302 average. Dennis Lamp (7-6) was third in the league in ERA (2.41) and Britt Burns (10-6) was fifth (2.64). Rich Dotson was 9-8 and Steve Trout was 8-7 but LaMarr Hoyt (9-3) had 10 saves in only 43 games. Attendance for the reduced season was a strong 946,651 but ended the White Sox streak of 1-million-plus seasons at four.

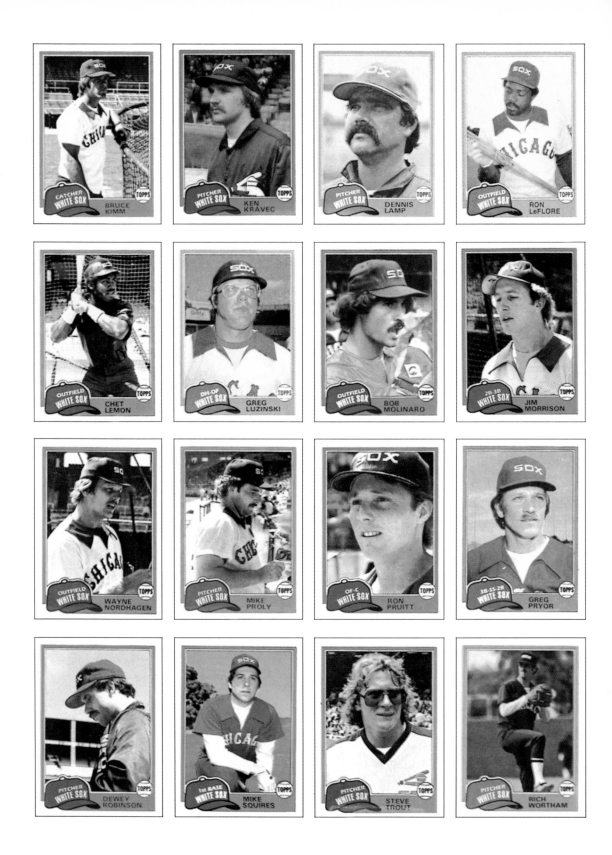

1982

Although snowed out for five days at the start of the season, the White Sox came out hot, winning the first eight, but then slowed down for a third-place finish (87-75), six games out. The win total was best since 1977. There were no hitters in the league's top 15 but Greg Luzinski hit .292 with 18 homers and 102 RBIs. Harold Baines (.271) had 25 homers and 105 RBIs. Steve Kemp (.286) added 19 homers and 98 RBIs. Rudy Law hit .318 with 36 stolen bases, displacing the controversial Ron LeFlore (.287) who had 28 thefts. LaMarr Hoyt (19-15) led the league in wins and had a 3.53 ERA (10th best). Hoyt, however, stumbled badly after a 9-0 start. Britt Burns (13-5), Rich Dotson (11-15), Jerry Koosman (11-7) and Dennis Lamp (11-8) were the other leading winners. Lamp also had five saves but Salome Barjas (6-6) was the star in the bullpen with 21.

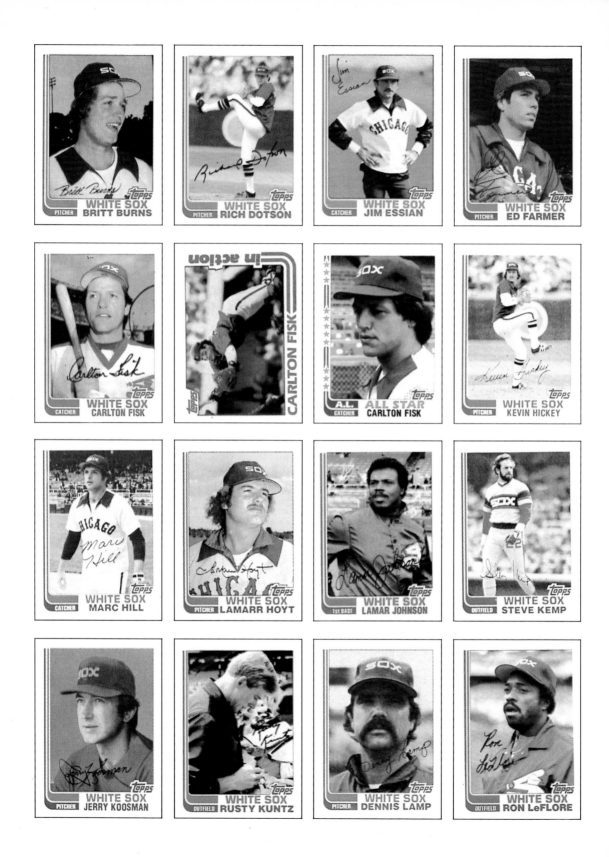

1983

For the first time since 1959, the White Sox were in post-season play after a surprisingly easy victory in the West with a 99-63 record and a margin of 20 games, a record for divisional play. Attendance set a record of 2,132,821 and they watched Rich Dotson roll to a 22-7 record with a 3.22 ERA (6th best in the league) and LaMarr Hoyt post a 24-10 mark. Tom Paciorek was the top hitter at .307 but the longball came from Carlton Fisk (.289) with 26 homers and 86 RBIs, Harold Baines (.280) with 20 homers and 99 RBIs, Greg Luzinski (.255) with 32 homers and 95 RBIs and Ron Kittle (.254) with a team-high 35 homers and 100 RBIs. Dennis Lamp (7-7) had 15 saves and Salome Barojas (3-3) had 12.

But the team that led the league with 800 runs during the season scored only 3 in 4 games against Baltimore in the pennant playoffs, losing 3 games to 1 and being outscored, 19 runs to 3. The White Sox won only the first game and that by a 1-0 score.

GREG LUZINSKI
DESIGNATED HITTER
WHITE SOX

SPARKY LYLE
PITCHER
WHITE SOX

★ SUPER VETERAN ★   SPARKY LYLE
1983   1967

TOM PACIOREK
1st BASE
WHITE SOX

AURELIO RODRIGUEZ
3rd BASE
WHITE SOX

MIKE SQUIRES
1st BASE
WHITE SOX

DICK TIDROW
PITCHER
WHITE SOX

STEVE TROUT
PITCHER
WHITE SOX

GREG WALKER
1st BASE
WHITE SOX

1982 BATTING & PITCHING LEADERS

LaMARR HOYT
3.53 ERA

GREG LUZINSKI
.292 BA

CHICAGO WHITE SOX

1984

In a remarkable turnabout, the rest of the West gained 30 games on the White Sox in a single season as the team that won by 20 games the year before finished fifth (74-88), 10 games out of the lead. Despite outstanding performances by several players including Harold Baines, Greg Walker, Greg Luzinski and Ron Kittle, the Sox never were serious contenders during the stretch. Baines hit .304 with 29 homers and 94 RBIs, Walker hit .294 with 24 homers and 75 RBIs, Luzinski batted .238 with 13 homers and 58 RBIs and Kittle, despite hitting only .215 with 100 total hits, slugged 32 homers and drove in 74 runs. One of the pre-season coups was the acquisition of righthander Tom Seaver from the Mets as compensation for the loss of free agent Dennis Lamp. Seaver led the pitchers with a 15-11 record and a 3.95 ERA. Rich Dotson was 14-15 with a 3.59, best on the team; LaMarr Hoyt was 13-18 and Floyd Bannister 14-11.

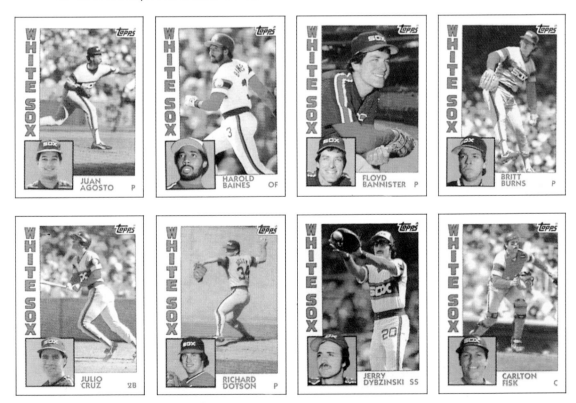

1985

After the shocking decline of the previous year, the White Sox made something of a comeback with an 85-77 record that moved them up to third, six games behind. Harold Baines, Carlton Fisk, Britt Burns and Tom Seaver were the big stars in the revival. Baines hit .309 with 22 homers and 113 RBIs (fourth highest in the league) and had 198 hits, fifth best in the league. Fisk hit only .238 but was second in the league in homers (37) and drove in 107 runs. Ron Kittle had another good power season with 26 homers and 58 RBIs but batted only .230. Burns led the pitchers with an 18-11 record (3.96 ERA) while Seaver was 16-11 with a 3.17 ERA. Veteran Bob James had the finest season of his career, posting an 8-7 record in relief with a 2.13 ERA and 32 saves (second highest in the league). Floyd Bannister had 198 strikeouts, best on the staff.

1986

By the end of April, the White Sox had fallen into sixth place in the West and stubbornly refused to budge higher than fifth despite a managerial change in June that ended Tony LaRussa's six-year tenure. LaRussa was dismissed on June 22 by general manager Ken Harrelson with the Sox 12 games under .500 (27-39) and Jim Fregosi took over. Under Fregosi, the club was 45-51 to finish fifth (72-90), 20 games out.

Harrelson himself was out in September, replaced by Tom Haller, but the primary reason for the team's performance, weak offense, remained. In 82 of 162 games, the Sox scored 3 runs or less and finished last in team batting (.247) and total bases. Harold Baines, though slowed by injury, was the batting star, hitting .296 with 21 homers and 88 RBIs. Rookie John Cangelosi (.235) set a league record for rookies with 50 stolen bases. Joe Cowley (11-11) was the team's leading winner and threw a no-hitter Sept. 19 at California. Floyd Bannister was 10-14 and Richard Dotson 10-17.

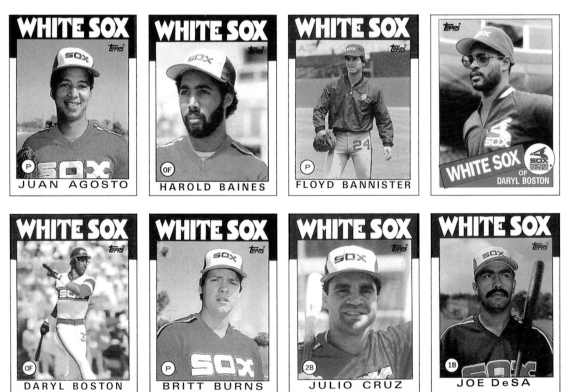

WHITE SOX — TONY LaRUSSA

WHITE SOX — RUDY LAW

WHITE SOX — BRYAN LITTLE

WHITE SOX — TIM LOLLAR

WHITE SOX — GENE NELSON

WHITE SOX — GENE NELSON

WHITE SOX — REID NICHOLS

WHITE SOX — LUIS SALAZAR

WHITE SOX — LUIS SALAZAR

WHITE SOX — TOM SEAVER

WHITE SOX — JOEL SKINNER

WHITE SOX — DAN SPILLNER

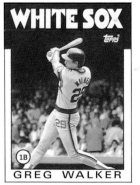

WHITE SOX — GREG WALKER

WHITE SOX LEADERS

Although many thought they were out of the race early in the season, the White Sox made a strong enough finish to pass two clubs and move up to fifth.

After the season, the White Sox rebuilding program continued when lefty Floyd Bannister was traded to Kansas City for a package of four fine young prospects. Bannister, with his 16-11 and 3.58 ERA, was the top pitcher for Chicago.

Among the highlights of the season was the power performance of 39-year-old Carlton Fisk. He became the oldest catcher in major league history to hit 20 or more homers in a season when he hit 23 while batting .256 and driving in 71 runs.

First baseman Greg Walker led the club in RBI with 94, hitting .256 with 27 homers.

Leftfielder Ivan Calderon was the top home run hitter with 28 while contributing a .293 average and 83 RBI.

Although hampered by injury, rightfielder Harold Baines produced a solid season, hitting .293 with 20 homers and 93 RBI. Centerfielder Ken Williams hit .281.

Leadoff man Gary Redus finished third in the league in stolen bases with 52 while shortstop Ozzie Guillen had 25 and Williams 21. Guillen hit .271.

In another off-season trade, pitcher Richard Dotson was traded to the New York Yankees for lefty slugger Dan Pasqua who hit 17 homers as a part-time player in New York.

Rookie Jack McDowell won all three of his decisions and had a 1.93 ERA after being called up in September.

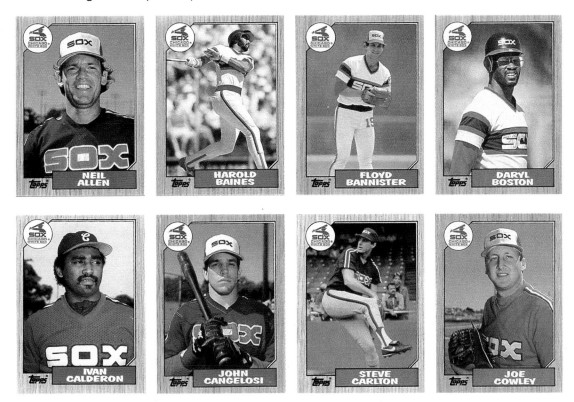

NEIL ALLEN   HAROLD BAINES   FLOYD BANNISTER   DARYL BOSTON

IVAN CALDERON   JOHN CANGELOSI   STEVE CARLTON   JOE COWLEY

JULIO CRUZ	JOEL DAVIS	BILL DAWLEY	JOSE DeLEON
RICHARD DOTSON	CARLTON FISK	JIM FREGOSI	OZZIE GUILLEN
JERRY HAIRSTON	RON HASSEY	DONNIE HILL	TIM HULETT
BOB JAMES	RON KARKOVICE	BILL LONG	STEVE LYONS

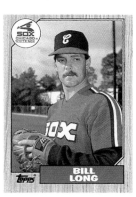

RUSS MORMAN

GENE NELSON

REID NICHOLS

GARY REDUS

JERRY ROYSTER

LUIS SALAZAR

DAVE SCHMIDT

RAY SEARAGE

BOBBY THIGPEN

GREG WALKER

JIM WINN

WHITE SOX LEADERS

1988

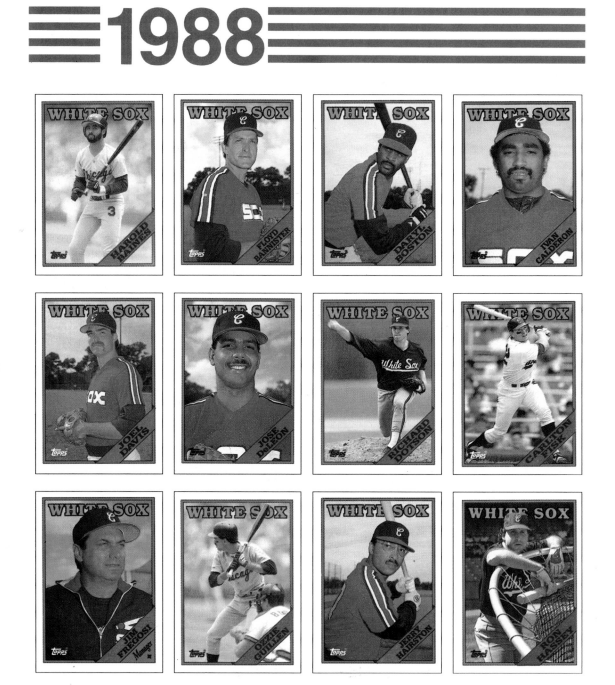

CARLTON FISK

CARLTON
FISK
CATCHER
WHITE SOX

Becoming the oldest catcher in major league history to hit 20 or more home runs in a season is the most recent in a long line of illustrious achievements for Carlton Fisk of the White Sox.

At 39, Fisk not only hit 23 homers last season, but also tied for second in the American League with 17 game-winning runs batted in and turned in a strong .460 slugging percentage.

Putting his career in perspective against the all-time greats, Fisk already ranks third among catchers in career home runs and is the only backstop in modern baseball history to have both 100 or more career home runs and 100 or more career stolen bases. He boasted 116 steals and 304 homers entering 1988.

From the time he arrived in the majors as the American League Rookie-of-the-Year in 1973, Fisk has been one of the truly outstanding performers in the game.

He earned nationwide acclaim in 1975 when his 12th-inning home run listed the Boston Red Sox to victory in the sixth game of the World Series against the Cincinnati Reds. The image of Fisk rooting his homer over the Fenway Park fence is one of baseball's most dramatic moments and is considered by many to have played a vital role in the resurgence of the game's attendance, which really began to soar the following year.

Many of Fisk's most enduring accomplishments have occurred since he joined the White Sox in 1981, giving instant recognition to the new ownership's desire to improve the club.

Although he had worn number "27" throughout his career, Fisk chose "72" when he joined the White Sox because, he said, "it represents a turnaround in my career."

In 1983, Fisk became the driving force when the White Sox captured the A.L. West. After a slow start, Fisk was moved to the second spot in the batting order and exploded. He finished with a career-best 26 homers and batted .319 over the second half of the season to earn strong support for the A.L. MVP, finishing third in the voting.

Fisk reached new levels in productivity during his 15th year in the majors in 1985 when he set career highs in homers (37) and RBIs (107). His home run outburst tied the White Sox single-season record set by Dick Allen in 1972. On September 6, at Texas, he hit two homers in a game for the third time that season and also drove in seven runs. Fisk finished second in the league in home runs and was named Chicago's Co-Player-of-the-Year by the baseball writers.

Fisk has become not only one of the pillars of the Sox but also one of the club's most popular players.

He also may be well on his way to a spot in the Hall of Fame as one of the greatest catchers in baseball history.

1951: Blue Back of Johnny Mize (50) lists for $25 . . . Red Back of Duke Snider (38) lists for $18 . . . Complete set of 9 Team Cards lists for $900 . . . Complete set of 11 Connie Mack All-Stars lists for $2750 with Babe Ruth and Lou Gehrig listing for $700 each . . . Current All-Stars of Jim Konstanty, Robin Roberts and Eddie Stanky list for $4000 each . . . Complete set lists for $14,250.

1952: Mickey Mantle (311) is unquestionably the most sought-after post-war gum card, reportedly valued at $6,500-plus . . . Ben Chapman (391) is photo of Sam Chapman . . . Complete set lists in excess of $36,000.

1953: Mickey Mantle (82) and Willie Mays (244) list for $1,500 each . . . Set features first TOPPS card of Hall-of-Famer Whitey Ford (207) and only TOPPS card of Hall-of-Famer Satchel Paige (220). Pete Runnels (219) is photo of Don Johnson . . . Complete set lists for $9,500.

1954: Ted Williams is depicted on two cards (1 and 250) . . . Set features rookie cards of Hank Aaron (128), Ernie Banks (94) and Al Kaline (201) . . . Card of Aaron lists for $650 . . . Card of Willie Mays (90) lists for $200 . . . Complete set lists for $5,500.

1955: Set features rookie cards of Sandy Koufax (123), Harmon Killebrew (124) and Roberto Clemente (164) . . . The Clemente and Willie Mays (194) cards list for $425 each . . .Complete set lists for $3,900.

1956: Set features rookie cards of Hall-of-Famers Will Harridge (1), Warren Giles (2), Walter Alston (8) and Luis Aparicio (292) . . . Card of Mickey Mantle (135) lists for $650 . . . Card of Willie Mays (130) lists for $125 . . . Complete set lists for $4,000 . . . The Team Cards are found both dated (1955) and undated and are valued at $15 (dated) and more . . . There are two unnumbered Checklist Cards valued high.

1957: Set features rookie cards of Don Drysdale (18), Frank Robinson (35) and Brooks Robinson (328) . . . A reversal of photo negative made Hank Aaron (20) appear as a left-handed batter . . . Card of Mickey Mantle (95) lists for $600 . . . Cards of Brooks Robinson and Sandy Koufax (302) list for $275 each . . . Complete set lists for $4,800.

1958: Set features first TOPPS cards of Casey Stengel (475) and Stan Musial (476) . . . Mike McCormick (37) is photo of Ray Monzant . . . Milt Bolling (188) is photo of Lou Berberet . . . Bob Smith (226) is photo of Bobby Gene Smith . . . Card of Mickey Mantle (150) lists for $400 . . . Card of Ted Williams (1) lists for $325 . . . Complete set lists for $4,800.

1959: In a notable error, Lou Burdette (440) is shown posing as a left-handed pitcher . . . Set features rookie card of Bob Gibson (514) . . . Ralph Lumenti (316) is photo of Camilo Pascual . . . Card of Gibson lists for $200 . . . Card of Mickey Mantle (10) lists for $300 . . . Complete set lists for $3,000.

1960: A run of 32 consecutively numbered rookie cards (117-148) includes the first card of Carl Yastrzemski (148) . . . J.C. Martin (346) is photo of Gary Peters . . . Gary Peters (407) is photo of J.C. Martin . . . Card of Yastrzemski lists for $150 . . . Card of Mickey Mantle (350) lists for $300 . . . Complete set lists for $2,600.

1961: The Warren Spahn All-Star (589) should have been numbered 587 . . . Set features rookie cards of Billy Williams (141) and Juan Marichal (417) . . . Dutch Dotterer (332) is photo of his brother, Tommy . . . Card of Mickey Mantle (300) lists for $200 . . . Card of Carl Yastrzemski (287) lists for $90 . . . Complete set lists for $3,600.

1962: Set includes special Babe Ruth feature (135-144) . . . some Hal Reniff cards numbered 139 should be 159 . . . Set features rookie card of Lou Brock (387) . . . Gene Freese (205) is shown posing as a left-handed batter . . . Card of Mickey Mantle (200) lists for $325 . . . Card of Carl Yastrzemski (425) lists for $125 . . . Complete set lists for $3,300.

1963: Set features rookie card of Pete Rose (537), which lists for $500-plus . . . Bob Uecker (126) is shown posing as a left-handed batter . . . Don Landrum (113) is photo of Ron Santo . . . Eli Grba (231) is photo of Ryne Duren . . . Card of Mickey Mantle (200) lists for $200 . . . Card of Lou Brock (472) lists for $75 . . . Complete set lists for $2,900.

1964: Set features rookie cards of Richie Allen (243), Tony Conigliaro (287) and Phil Niekro (541) . . . Lou Burdette is again shown posing as a left-handed pitcher . . . Bud Bloomfield (532) is photo of Jay Ward . . . Card of Pete Rose (125) lists for $150 . . . Card of Mickey Mantle (50) lists for $175 . . . Complete set lists for $1,600.

1965: Set features rookie cards of Dave Johnson (473), Steve Carlton (477) and Jim Hunter (526) . . . Lew Krausse (462) is photo of Pete Lovrich . . . Gene Freese (492) is again shown posing as a left-handed batter . . . Cards of Carlton and Pete Rose (207) list for $135 . . . Card of Mickey Mantle (350) lists for $300 . . . Complete set lists for $800.

1966: Set features rookie card of Jim Palmer (126) . . . For the third time (see 1962 and 1965) Gene Freese (319) is shown posing as a left-handed batter . . . Dick Ellsworth (447) is photo of Ken Hubbs (died February 13, 1964) . . . Card of Gaylord Perry (598) lists for $175 . . . Card of Willie McCovey (550) lists for $80 . . . Complete set lists for $2,500.

1967: Set features rookie cards of Rod Carew (569) and Tom Seaver (581) . . . Jim Fregosi (385) is shown posing as a left-handed batter . . . George Korince (72) is photo of James Brown but was later corrected on a second Korince card (526) . . . Card of Carew lists for $150 . . . Card of Maury Wills (570) lists for $65 . . . Complete set lists for $2,500.

1968: Set features rookie cards of Nolan Ryan (177) and Johnny Bench (247) . . . The special feature of The Sporting News All-Stars (361-380) includes eight players in the Hall of Fame . . . Card of Ryan lists for $135 . . . Card of Bench lists for $125 . . . Complete set lists for $1,200.

1969: Set features rookie card of Reggie Jackson (260) . . . There are two poses each for Clay Dalrymple (151) and Donn Clendenon (208) . . . Aurelio Rodriguez (653) is photo of Lenny Garcia (Angels' bat boy) . . . Card of Mickey Mantle (500) lists for $150 . . . Card of Jackson lists for $175 . . . Complete set lists for $1,200.

1970: Set features rookie cards of Vida Blue (21), Thurman Munson (189) and Bill Buckner (286) . . . Also included are two deceased players Miguel Fuentes (88) and Paul Edmondson (414) who died after cards went to press . . . Card of Johnny Bench (660) lists for $75 . . . Card of Pete Rose (580) lists for $75 . . . Complete set lists for $1,000.

1971: Set features rookie card of Steve Garvey (341) . . . the final series (644-752) is found in lesser quantity and includes rookie card (664) of three pitchers named Reynolds (Archie, Bob and Ken) . . . Card of Garvey lists for $65 . . . Card of Pete Rose (100) lists for $45 . . . Complete set lists for $1,000.

1972: There were 16 cards featuring photos of players in their boyhood years . . . Dave Roberts (91) is photo of Danny Coombs . . . Brewers Rookie Card (162) includes photos of Darrell Porter and Jerry Bell, which were reversed . . . Cards of Steve Garvey (686) and Rod Carew (695) list for $60 . . . Card of Pete Rose (559) lists for $50 . . . Complete set lists for $1,000.

1973: A special Home Run Card (1) depicted Babe Ruth, Hank Aaron and Willie Mays . . . Set features rookie card of Mike Schmidt (615) listing for $175 . . . Joe Rudi (360) is photo of Gene Tenace . . . Card of Pete Rose (130) lists for $18 . . . Card of Reggie Jackson (255) lists for $12.50 . . . Complete set lists for $600.

1974: Set features 15 San Diego Padres cards printed as "Washington, N.L." due to report of franchise move, later corrected . . . Also included was a 44-card Traded Series which updated team changes . . . Set features rookie card of Dave Winfield (456) . . . Card of Mike Schmidt (283) lists for $35 . . . Card of Winfield lists for $25 . . . Complete set lists for $325.

1975: Herb Washington (407) is the only card ever published with position "designated runner," featuring only base-running statistics . . . Set features rookie cards of Robin Yount (223), George Brett (228), Jim Rice (616), Gary Carter (620) and Keith Hernandez (623) . . . Don Wilson (455) died after cards went to press (January 5, 1975) . . . Card of Brett lists for $50 . . . Cards of Rice and Carter list for $35 . . . Complete set lists for $475 . . . TOPPS also tested the complete 660-card series in a smaller size (2¼" x 3 1/8") in certain areas of USA in a limited supply . . . Complete set of "Mini-Cards" lists for $700.

1976: As in 1974 there was a 44-card Traded Series . . . Set features five Father & Son cards (66-70) and ten All-Time All-Stars (341-350) . . . Card of Pete Rose (240) lists for $15 . . . Cards of Jim Rice (340), Gary Carter (441) and George Brett (19) list for $12 . . . Complete set lists for $225.

1977: Set features rookie cards of Andre Dawson (473) and Dale Murphy (476) . . . Reuschel Brother Combination (634) shows the two (Paul and Rick) misidentified . . . Dave Collins (431) is photo of Bob Jones . . . Card of Murphy lists for $65 . . . Card of Pete Rose (450) lists for $8.50 . . . Complete set lists for $250.

1978: Record Breakers (1-7) feature Lou Brock, Sparky Lyle, Willie McCovey, Brooks Robinson, Pete Rose, Nolan Ryan and Reggie Jackson . . . Set features rookie cards of Jack Morris (703), Lou Whitaker (704), Paul Molitor/Alan Trammell (707), Lance Parrish (708) and Eddie Murray (36) . . . Card of Murray lists for $35 . . . Card of Parrish lists for $35 . . . Complete set lists for $200.

1979: Bump Wills (369) was originally shown with Blue Jays affiliation but later corrected to Rangers . . . Set features rookie cards of Ozzie Smith (116), Pedro Guerrero (719), Lonnie Smith (722) and Terry Kennedy (724) . . . Larry Cox (489) is photo of Dave Rader . . . Card of Dale Murphy (39) lists for $8 . . . Cards of Ozzie Smith and Eddie Murray (640) list for $7.50 . . . Complete set lists for $135.

1980: Highlights (1-6) feature Hall-of-Famers Lou Brock, Carl Yastrzemski, Willie McCovey and Pete Rose . . . Set features rookie cards of Dave Stieb (77), Rickey Henderson (482) and Dan Quisenberry (667) . . . Card of Henderson lists for $28 . . . Card of Dale Murphy (274) lists for $5.50 . . . Complete set lists for $135.

1981: Set features rookie cards of Fernando Valenzuela (302), Kirk Gibson (315), Harold Baines (347) and Tim Raines (479) . . . Jeff Cox (133) is photo of Steve McCatty . . . John Littlefield (489) is photo of Mark Riggins . . . Card of Valenzuela lists for $7.50 . . . Card of Raines lists for $9 . . . Complete set lists for $80.

1982: Pascual Perez (383) printed with no position on front lists for $35, later corrected . . . Set features rookie cards of Cal Ripken (21), Jesse Barfield (203), Steve Sax (681) and Kent Hrbek (766) . . . Dave Rucker (261) is photo of Roger Weaver . . . Steve Bedrosian (502) is photo of Larry Owen . . . Card of Ripken lists for $12.50 . . . Cards of Barfield and Sax list for $5 . . . Complete set lists for $75.

1983: Record Breakers (1-6) feature Tony Armas, Rickey Henderson, Greg Minton, Lance Parrish, Manny Trillo and John Wathan . . . A series of Super Veterans features early and current photos of 34 leading players . . . Set features rookie cards of Tony Gwynn (482) and Wade Boggs (498) . . . Card of Boggs lists for $32 . . . Card of Gwynn lists for $16 . . . Complete set lists for $85.

1984: Highlights (1-6) salute eleven different players . . . A parade of superstars is included in Active Leaders (701-718) . . . Set features rookie card of Don Mattingly (8) listing for $35 . . . Card of Darryl Strawberry (182) lists for $10 . . . Complete set lists for $85.

1985: A Father & Son Feature (131-143) is again included . . . Set features rookie cards of Scott Bankhead (393), Mike Dunne (395), Shane Mack (398), John Marzano (399), Oddibe McDowell (400), Mark McGwire (401), Pat Pacillo (402), Cory Snyder (403) and Billy Swift (404) as part of salute to 1984 USA Baseball Team (389-404) that participated in Olympic Games plus rookie cards of Roger Clemens (181) and Eric Davis (627) . . . Card of McGwire lists for $20 . . . Card of Davis lists for $18 . . . Card of Clemens lists for $11 . . . Complete set lists for $95.

1986: Set includes Pete Rose Feature (2-7), which reproduces each of Rose's TOPPS cards from 1963 thru 1985 (four per card) . . . Bob Rodgers (141) should have been numbered 171 . . . Ryne Sandberg (690) is the only card with TOPPS logo omitted . . . Complete set lists for $24.

1987: Record Breakers (1-7) feature Roger Clemens, Jim Deshaies, Dwight Evans, Davey Lopes, Dave Righetti, Ruben Sierra and Todd Worrell . . . Jim Gantner (108) is shown with Brewers logo reversed . . . Complete set lists for $22.

1988: Record Breakers (1-7) include Vince Coleman, Don Mattingly, Mark McGwire, Eddie Murray, Phil & Joe Niekro, Nolan Ryan and Benny Santiago. Al Leiter (18) was originally shown with photo of minor leaguer Steve George and later corrected. Complete set lists for $20.00.

Pitching Record & Index

PLAYER	G	IP	W	L	R	ER	SO	BB	GS	CG	SHO	SV	ERA
ABARBANEL, MICKEY					No major league statistics								
ACKLEY, FRITZ	5	19	1	0			17	11	4	0	0	0	4.26
ACOSTA, CY	107	187	13	9			109	77	1	0	0	27	2.65
AGOSTO, JUAN	171	190.1	9	10	104	93	110	86	1	0	0	16	4.40
ALLEN, LLOYD	159	297	9	25			194	196	19	0	0	22	4.70
ALLEN, NEIL	367	793.2	53	58	356	322	508	344	46	7	5	75	3.65
ALOMA, LUIS	116	235	18	3			115	111	1	1	1	15	3.45
ANDERSON, LARRY	16	41	2	3			23	22	1	0	0	0	5.71
ARIAS, RUDY	34	44	2	0			28	20	0	0	0	2	4.09
ARRIGO, GERRY	194	620	35	40			433	291	80	9	3	2	4.14
BAHNSEN, STAN	574	2527	146	149			1359	924	327	73	16	20	3.61
BALDWIN, DAVE	176	225	6	11			164	89	0	0	0	22	3.08
BANNISTER, FLOYD	300	1832.1	101	117	908	820	1405	680	284	49	14	3	4.03
BARRIOS, FRANCISCO	129	718	38	38			323	246	102	27	4	3	4.15
BAUMANN, FRANK	244	798	45	38			384	300	78	19	4	13	4.11
BAUMGARTEN, ROSS	90	496	22	36			222	211	84	10	6	0	3.99
BEARDEN, GENE	193	789	45	38			259	435	84	29	7	1	3.96
BELL, GARY	519	2015	121	117			1378	842	233	71	9	51	3.68
BOLLO, GREG	18	30	0	1			20	12	1	0	0	2	3.30
BRADLEY, TOM	183	1018	55	61			691	311	151	27	10	2	3.72
BRENNAN, TOM	52	187	8	7			85	35	16	2	1	2	3.90
BRETT, KEN	349	1526	83	85			807	562	184	51	8	11	3.93
BROSNAN, JIM	385	832	55	47			507	312	47	7	2	67	3.54
BROWN, HAL	358	1680	85	92			710	389	211	47	13	11	3.81
BROWN, WINSTON					No major league statistics								
BRUSSTAR, WARREN	340	484.1	28	16			273	183	0	0	0	14	3.51
BURNS, BRITT	193	1095	70	60			734	362	161	39	11	3	3.66
BUZHARDT, JOHN	326	1489	71	96			678	457	200	44	15	3	3.67
BYRD, HARRY	187	827	46	54			381	355	108	33	8	9	4.35
BYRNE, TOMMY	281	1363	85	69			766	1037	170	65	12	12	4.11
CADORE, LEON	192	1257	68	72			445	289	147	83	10	4	3.14
CAIN, BOB	140	629	37	44			249	316	89	27	4	3	4.49
CARLOS, CISCO	73	235	11	18			119	79	36	1	1	8	3.75
CARLTON, STEVE	705	5054.2	323	229	2000	1749	4040	1742	687	251	55	2	3.11
CARROLL, CLAY	731	1353	96	73			681	442	28	1	1	143	2.94
CHAKALES, BOB	171	420	15	25			187	225	23	3	1	10	4.54
CLARK, BRYAN	158	478.1	18	23			243	241	37	4	1	4	4.23
CONNELLY, BILL	25	66	6	2			34	53	7	0	0	0	6.95
CONSUEGRA, SANDY	248	810	51	32			193	246	71	24	5	26	3.37
COONEY, JOHNNY	159	796	34	44			224	223	76	44	7	0	3.72
CORREA, ED	37	212.2	13	14	111	103	199	137	33	2	0	0	4.36
COWLEY, JOE	90	457.2	33	21	217	199	327	215	72	8	1	0	3.91
CRIDER, JERRY	53	120	5	7			56	49	9	0	0	2	4.50
DAL CANTON, BRUCE	316	930	51	49			485	491	83	9	2	19	3.68
DAVIS, JOEL	31	176.2	7	8	98	88	91	77	30	1	0	0	4.48
DAWLEY, BILL	203	356.1	22	20	123	114	221	122	10	0	0	23	2.88
DEBUSSCHERE, DAVE	36	102	3	4			61	57	10	1	1	4	2.91
DELEON, JOSE	98	558.1	21	43	261	240	499	287	82	10	3	4	3.87
DERRINGTON, JIM	21	43	0	2			17	35	6	0	0	0	5.23
DOBSON, JOE	414	2172	137	103			992	851	273	112	22	18	3.62
DONOVAN, DICK	345	2020	122	99			880	495	273	101	25	5	3.66
DORISH, HARRY	323	835	45	43			332	301	40	13	2	44	3.83
DOTSON, RICHARD	206	1294.2	83	76	639	577	704	510	202	42	9	0	4.01
DRABOWSKY, MOE	589	1640	88	105			1162	702	154	30	6	55	3.71
EDDY, DON	29	35	0	2			23	25	0	0	0	2	2.31
EDMONDSON, PAUL	14	88	1	6			46	39	13	1	0	0	3.68

PLAYER	G	IP	W	L	R	ER	SO	BB	GS	CG	SHO	SV	ERA
ELLIS, SAMMY	229	1004	63	58			677	378	140	35	3	18	4.15
FARMER, BILLY					No major league statistics								
FARMER, ED	370	624	30	43			395	345	21	0	0	75	4.30
FERRARESE, DON	183	507	19	36			350	295	50	12	2	5	3.99
FILSON, PETE	126	316.2	14	13			160	121	24	1	0	4	3.95
FIREOVID, STEVE	28	64.2	2	1	26	24	27	15	5	0	0	0	3.34
FISCHER, BILL	281	832	45	58			313	210	78	16	2	13	4.34
FISHER, EDDIE	690	1541	85	70			812	438	63	7	2	81	3.40
FISHER, JACK	400	1977	86	139			1017	605	265	63	9	9	4.06
FORNIELES, MIEK	432	1156	63	64			576	421	76	20	4	55	3.96
FORSTER, TERRY	614	1105.1	54	65	454	397	791	457	39	5	0	127	3.23
FRAILING, KEN	116	218	10	16			136	82	19	1	1	8	3.96
FROST, DAVE	99	549.2	33	37			222	174	84	16	3	23	4.11
GARCIA, MIKE	428	2176	142	97			1117	719	281	111	27	0	3.26
GEDDES, JIM	11	26	0	0			10	24	2	0	0	0	4.50
GIBSON, JOEL					No major league statistics								
GLEATON, JERRY DON	75	154.2	6	10			62	65	16	1	0	3	5.06
GOGOLEWSKI, BILL	144	502	15	24			301	200	44	6	1	9	4.02
GOSSAGE, RICH	725	1482.1	101	89	531	473	1275	592	37	16	0	278	2.87
GRANGER, WAYNE	451	640	35	35			303	201	0	0	0	108	3.14
GRISSOM, MARV	356	810	47	45			459	343	52	12	3	58	3.41
GUMPERT, RANDY	261	1052	51	59			352	346	113	47	6	17	4.17
HACKER, WARREN	306	1283	62	89			557	320	157	47	6	17	4.21
HAMILTON, DAVE	301	703	39	41			434	317	57	4	1	31	3.85
HAMILTON, JACK	218	612	32	40			357	238	65	8	1	20	4.53
HAMILTON, STEVE	421	662	40	31			531	214	17	3	1	42	3.06
HARRIST, EARL	132	383	12	28			162	193	24	2	0	10	4.34
HARSHMAN, JACK	217	1168	69	65			741	539	155	61	12	4	3.51
HAYNES, JOE	379	1580	76	82			475	620	147	53	5	21	4.01
HENDERSON, JOE	16	35	3	2			27	25	3	0	0	0	6.69
HERBERT, RAY	407	1883	104	107			864	571	236	75	13	15	4.01
HICKEY, KEVIN	124	142.2	5	8			63	59	0	0	0	14	3.53
HIGGINS, DENNIS	241	205	22	23			179	134	2	0	0	46	3.78
HINTON, RICH	116	250	9	17			152	91	13	0	0	3	4.86
HOFFMAN, GUY	58	74	5	5			44	42	2	1	0	3	4.14
HOLCOMBE, KEN	99	374	18	32			118	170	48	18	2	2	3.99
HORLEN, JOEL	361	2003	116	117			1065	554	290	59	18	4	3.55
HOWARD, BRUCE	120	529	26	31			349	239	75	7	4	1	3.18
HOWARD, FRED	28	68	1	5			36	32	6	0	0	0	3.57
HOWELL, H. 'DIXIE'	115	226	19	15			99	103	2	0	0	19	3.78
HOYT, LAMARR	244	1311.1	98	68	637	582	681	279	172	48	8	10	3.99
HUGHES, JIM R.	172	297	15	13	162	144	165	152	1	0	0	39	3.82
JAMES, BOB	236	353	20	20			306	140	2	0	0	63	3.67
JANESKI, GERRY	62	281	11	23			105	104	46	4	1	4	4.71
JEFFERSON, JESSE	237	1086	39	81			522	520	144	25	4	4	4.81
JOHN, TOMMY	682	4279.2	264	210	1781	1536	2083	1144	625	159	45	4	3.23
JOHNSON, BART	185	810	43	51			520	348	97	22	6	17	3.93
JOHNSON, CONNIE	123	716	40	39			497	257	100	34	8	4	3.44
JOHNSON, DON	198	631	27	38			262	285	70	17	4	12	4.78
JONES, AL	27	28.2	2	1			19	16	0	0	0	5	3.77
JONES, STEVE	42	80	5	7			59	43	3	0	0	2	4.50
JOYCE, MIKE	31	54	1	2			16	22	1	0	0	0	4.33
JUDSON, HOWIE	207	615	17	37			204	319	48	8	1	14	4.29
KAAT, JIM	898	4527.2	283	237			2461	1083	625	180	31	18	3.45
KEALEY, STEVE	139	214	8	5			126	69	4	1	0	11	3.71
KEEGAN, BOB	135	646	40	36			198	233	87	29	6	5	3.65

PLAYER	G	IP	W	L	R	ER	SO	BB	GS	CG	SHO	SV	ERA
KEMMERER, RUSS	302	1066	43	59			505	389	109	24	2	8	4.47
KENNEDY, BILL	172	465	15	32			256	289	45	6	1	11	4.70
KERN, JIM	395	754.2	52	55			637	416	14	1	0	88	3.11
KINDER, ELLIS	484	1480	102	71			749	539	122	56	10	102	3.43
KIRKWOOD, DON	120	375	18	23			194	135	37	7	0	0	4.37
KLAGES, FRED	14	61	5	4			23	23	12	0	0	0	3.25
KNAPP, CHRIS	122	603	36	32			355	250	99	15	2	0	5.00
KOOSMAN, JERRY	612	3839.1	222	209			2556	1198	527	140	33	17	3.36
KRAVEC, KEN	160	859	43	56			557	404	128	24	6	1	4.46
KRETLOW, LOU	199	786	27	47			450	522	104	22	3	1	4.87
KREUTZER, FRANK	78	210	8	18			151	109	32	2	1	1	4.41
KUCEK, JACK	59	207	7	16			121	111	27	3	0	2	5.09
KUZAVA, BOB	213	862	49	44			446	415	99	34	6	13	4.05
LAGROW, LERRIN	309	778	34	55			375	312	67	19	2	54	4.12
LAMABE, JACK	285	710	33	41			434	238	49	7	3	15	4.25
LAMP, DENNIS	396	1353.2	74	76	670	587	590	411	157	21	7	33	3.90
LAPALME, PAUL	253	616	24	45			277	272	51	10	2	14	4.42
LAPOINT, DAVE	191	898.2	46	49	453	396	532	358	131	5	1	2	3.97
LARSEN, DON	412	1549	81	91			849	725	171	44	11	23	3.78
LARY, FRANK	350	2162	128	116			1099	616	292	126	21	11	3.49
LATMAN, BARRY	344	1219	59	68			829	489	134	28	10	16	3.91
LAZAR, DAN	17	34	0	1			20	15	4	0	0	0	5.56
LEMON, BOB	460	2849	207	128			1277	1251	350	188	31	22	3.23
LEMONDS, DAVE	33	100	4	8			69	43	19	0	0	0	2.97
LITTLEFIELD, DICK	243	761	33	54			495	413	83	16	0	9	4.72
LOCKER, BOB	576	878	57	39			577	257	0	0	0	95	2.76
LOLLAR, TIM	199	906	47	52	459	430	600	480	131	9	4	4	4.27
LOPAT, EDDIE	340	2439	166	112			859	650	318	164	27	3	3.21
LOWN, TURK	504	1031	55	61			574	590	49	10	1	73	4.12
LYLE, SPARKY	899	1390.2	99	76			873	481	0	0	0	238	2.88
MAGNUSON, JIM	36	102	2	7			40	41	1	0	0	1	4.59
MAHONEY, BOB	36	91	2	5			34	50	4	0	0	2	4.95
MARTIN, MORRIE	250	604	38	34			245	251	42	8	1	15	4.29
MARTINEZ, SILVIO	107	583	31	32			230	237	87	14	4	0	3.87
MARTZ, RANDY	68	290.2	17	19			78	100	45	2	1	7	3.78
MCBRIDE, KEN	151	808	40	50			503	353	122	28	7	2	3.79
MCGLOTHEN, LYNN	318	1498	86	93			939	572	201	41	13	3	3.98
MCGLOTHLIN, JIM	256	1300	67	77			544	418	201	36	8	2	3.61
MCLISH, CAL	352	1609	92	92			713	552	209	57	5	6	4.01
MCMAHON, DON	874	1312	90	68			1003	579	2	0	0	153	2.96
MILLER, BOB L.	694	1552	69	81			895	608	99	7	0	52	3.37
MONTEAGUDO, AURELIO	75	131	3	7			58	62	7	0	0	4	5.08
MOORE, BARRY	140	600	26	37			278	300	99	8	1	3	4.15
MOORE, RAY	365	1073	63	59			612	560	105	24	5	46	4.06
MOSSI, DON	460	1548	101	80			932	385	165	55	8	50	3.43
MURA, STEVE	167	528.2	30	34	287	267	360	289	83	6	1	5	3.99
NELSON, GENE	160	636	28	32	29	25	305	229	59	6	2	4	4.55
NELSON, ROGER	135	636	29	29			371	190	77	20	7	4	3.06
NIEMANN, RANDY	116	194.2	6	8	107	98	101	75	10	1	0	2	4.53
NYMAN, GERRY	30	110	6	7			69	57	19	3	1	0	4.58
O'TOOLE, DENNIS	15	30	0	0			22	10	0	0	0	0	5.10
O'TOOLE, JIM	270	1615	98	84			1039	546	238	58	8	3	3.57
OSBORN, DAN	24	58	3	5			37	38	8	0	0	0	4.50
OSINKSI, DAN	324	590	29	28			400	264	21	1	0	18	3.30
OSTEEN, CLAUDE	541	3460	196	195			1612	940	488	140	40	2	3.30
OTTEN, JIM	64	118	4	6			75	67	5	0	0	1	5.49
PATTERSON, REGGIE	14	31.2	1	4			17	14	4	0	0	0	7.96
PERZANOWSKI, STAN	37	143	5	11			70	60	16	2	0	0	5.10
PETERS, GARY	359	2081	124	103			1420	706	286	79	23	5	3.25
PHILLIPS, TAYLOR	147	439	16	22			233	211	45	9	1	6	4.82
PIERCE, BILL	585	3305	211	169			1999	1178	432	193	38	32	3.27
PITLOCK, SKIP	59	193	7	8			124	103	20	1	0	1	4.52
PIZARRO, JUAN	488	2035	131	105			1520	888	245	79	17	28	3.43
POLLET, HOWIE	403	2106	131	116			934	745	277	116	25	20	3.51
PRIDDY, BOB	249	535	24	38			294	198	29	3	0	18	4.00
PROLY, MIKE	267	546	22	29			185	195	18	2	0	22	3.23
QUALTERS, TOM	34	52	0	0			20	26	0	0	0	0	5.71
RAYMOND, CLAUDE	449	720	46	53			497	225	7	2	0	83	3.66
REED, RON	751	2475.1	146	140			1481	633	236	55	8	103	3.46
REGAN, PHIL	551	1373	96	81			743	447	105	20	3	92	3.83
RENKO, STEVE	451	2493.	134	146			1455	1010	365	57	9	6	4.00
RIBANT, DENNIS	149	519	24	29			241	126	56	12	2	9	3.87
ROBERGE, BERT	125	190.1	12	8			99	70	0	0	0	9	3.64
ROBINSON, DEWEY	30	53	2	2			35	28	0	0	0	2	4.08
ROGOVIN, SAUL	150	885	48	48			388	308	121	43	9	2	4.06
ROMO, VICENTE	335	645.2	32	33			416	281	32	4	1	52	3.36
RUDOLPH, DON	124	450	18	32			182	102	57	10	2	3	4.00
RUSH, BOB	417	2409	127	152			1244	789	321	118	16	8	3.65
SAWYER, RICK	78	206.2	9	9			85	98	20	2	0	6	4.40
SCARBERY, RANDY	60	130	3	10			63	41	5	0	0	4	4.50
SCARBOROUGH, RAY	318	1429	80	85			564	611	168	59	9	14	4.13
SCHEULER, RON	291	914	40	48			563	393	86	13	2	11	4.08
SCHMIDT, DAVE	291	436.1	23	28	179	154	270	119	14	1	1	34	3.18
SCHREIBER, PAUL	12	20	0	2			5	10	0	0	0	0	4.05
SCORE, HERB	150	858	55	46			837	573	127	47	11	3	3.36
SEARAGE, RAY	126	164.1	7	6			117	85	0	0	0	3	3.40
SEAVER, TOM	656	4782	311	205	1674	1511	3640	1390	647	231	61	1	2.84
SECRIST, DON	28	55	0	1			32	26	0	0	0	0	5.80
SHAW, BOB	430	1779	108	98			880	511	223	55	15	32	3.52
SHIPLEY, JOE	36	44	0	1			23	35	1	0	0	0	5.93
SIMA, AL	100	308	11	21			111	132	30	4	0	4	4.62
SISK, TOMMIE	316	928	40	49			441	358	99	19	4	10	3.92
SOLOMON, EDDIE	191	718	36	42			337	247	95	8	0	4	4.00
SPILLNER, DAN	556	1493	75	89			878	605	123	19	3	50	4.21
STALEY, GERRY	640	1981	134	111			727	529	186	58	9	61	3.70
STANGE, LEE	359	1216	62	61			718	344	115	32	8	21	3.56
STANTON, MIKE	242	343.1	12	19			275	153	3	0	0	30	4.40
STODDARD, TIM	459	692	35	30	257	238	459	292	0	0	0	65	4.29
STONE, DEAN	215	687	29	39			380	373	85	19	7	12	3.82
STONE, STEVE	320	1789	107	93			1065	716	269	43	7	0	4.47
STRIKER, JAKE	3	1	0	0			6	0	0	0	0	0	3.96
SURKONT, MAX	236	1194	61	76			571	481	149	53	7	8	4.38
TALBOT, FRED	195	854	38	56			449	334	126	12	4	4	4.12
TATUM, KEN	176	283	16	12			156	117	2	0	0	52	2.93
THIGPEN, BOBBY	20	35.2	2	0	7	7	20	12	0	0	0	7	1.77
TIDROW, DICK	620	1747	100	94			967	572	138	33	5	55	3.63
TORREALBA, PABLO	111	240	6	13			113	104	13	4	2	5	3.26
TROUT, STEVE	242	1294	74	75	648	567	566	466	200	29	5	0	3.94
TRUCKS, VIRGIL	517	2684	177	135			1534	1088	328	124	33	30	3.38
UPSHAW, CECIL	348	563	34	36			323	177	0	0	0	86	3.13
VALENTINETTI, VITO	108	257	13	14			94	122	15	3	0	3	4.73
VERHOEVEN, JOHN	99	204	3	8			90	63	0	0	0	3	3.79
VUCKOVICH, PETE	280	1422	91	65			870	534	180	38	8	10	3.68
WEAVER, FLOYD	85	155	4	5			108	73	5	0	0	1	5.23
WEHRMEISTER, DAVE	53	118	2	7			64	74	10	0	0	0	6.41
WIDMAR, AL	114	389	13	30			143	176	42	12	1	5	5.21
WIGHT, BILL	347	1562	77	99			574	714	198	66	15	5	3.95
WILHELM, HOYT	1070	2253	143	122			1610	778	52	20	5	227	2.52
WILLOUGHBY, JIM	238	551	26	36			250	145	28	8	1	34	3.79
WILLS, TED	83	186	8	11			133	97	13	2	0	5	5.52

PLAYER	G	IP	W	L	R	ER	SO	BB	GS	CG	SHO	SV	ERA
WILSON, JIM	257	1540	86	89			692	608	217	75	19	2	4.01
WINN, JIM	96	193.1	7	11			106	84	10	0	0	4	4.47
WOOD, WILBUR	651	2684	164	156	106	96	1411	724	297	114	24	57	3.24
WORTHAM, RICH	84	355	21	23			189	182	51	7	0	1	4.89
WORTHINGTON, AL	602	1245	75	82			834	527	69	11	3	110	3.39
WYATT, WHITLOW	360	1762	106	95			872	642	210	97	17	13	3.78
WYNN, EARLY	691	4566	300	244			2334	1775	612	290	49	15	3.54
WYNNE, BILLY	42	188	8	11			97	78	30	6	1	0	4.31
ZANNI, DOM	111	182	9	6			148	85	3	0	0	10	3.81

Batting Record & Index

PLAYER	G	AB	R	H	2B	3B	HR	RBI	SB	SLG	BB	SO	AVG
ABRAMS, CAL	567	1611	257	433	64	19	32	138	12	.392	304	290	.269
ADAIR, JERRY	1165	4019	378	1022	163	19	57	366	29	.347	208	499	.254
ADAMS, BOBBY	1281	4019	591	1082	188	49	37	303	67	.368	414	447	.269
AGEE, TOMMIE	1129	3912	558	999	170	27	130	433	167	.412	342	918	.255
ALLEN, HANK	389	881	104	212	27	6	6	57	15	.312	49	128	.241
ALLEN, RICHIE	1749	6332	1099	1848	320	79	351	1119	133	.534	894	1556	.292
ALMON, BILL	1148	3230	376	826	132	25	36	290	127	.346	238	604	.256
ALOMAR, SANDY	1481	4760	558	1168	126	19	13	282	227	.271	302	482	.245
ALVARADO, LUIS	463	1160	116	248	43	4	11	84	11	.271	47	160	.214
ANDREWS, MIKE	893	3116	441	803	140	4	66	316	19	.369	458	390	.258
APARICIO, LUIS	2599	10230	1335	2677	394	92	83	791	506	.343	735	742	.262
AVERILL, EARL	449	1031	137	249	41	4	44	159	3	.409	162	220	.242
BAINES, HAROLD	992	3754	492	1077	182	38	140	589	29	.468	263	539	.287
BAKER, FLOYD	874	2819	285	573	76	13	1	196	23	.278	382	165	.251
BANNISTER, ALAN	972	3007	430	811	143	28	19	288	108	.355	292	319	.270
BATTEY, EARL	1141	3586	393	969	150	13	104	449	6	.409	421	470	.270
BATTS, MATT	546	1605	163	432	95	11	26	219	6	.391	143	163	.269
BAUMER, JIM	18	34	4	7	1	0	1	2	0	.294	2	10	.206
BEARD, TED	194	474	80	94	11	6	9	35	16	.285	78	107	.198
BELL, KEVIN	297	726	74	161	22	9	13	64	5	.285	70	165	.222
BERNAZARD, TONY	925	3181	450	841	151	28	61	342	102	.387	373	523	.264
BERRY, KEN	1383	4156	422	1053	150	23	58	343	45	.342	298	569	.253
BEVAN, HAL	15	24	2	7	0	0	0	1	2	.417	0	3	.292
BLOMBERG, RON	461	1333	184	391	67	8	52	224	6	.473	140	134	.293
BONDS, BOBBY	1849	7043	1258	1886	302	66	332	1024	461	.471	914	1757	.268
BONILLA, BOBBY	138	426	55	109	16	4	8	43	3	.333	62	88	.256
BOONE, RAY	1373	4589	645	1260	162	46	151	737	21	.429	608	463	.275
BORGMANN, GLENN	474	1294	139	296	42	4	16	151	4	.304	191	191	.229
BOSLEY, THAD	587	1276	152	353	37	17	17	121	43	.363	119	213	.277
BOSTON, DARYL	186	514	57	120	27	5	8	40	23	.352	39	97	.233
BOYD, BOB	693	1936	253	567	81	23	19	175	9	.388	167	114	.293
BOYER, KEN	2034	7455	1104	2143	318	68	282	1141	105	.462	713	1017	.287
BRADFORD, BUDDY	697	1603	224	363	50	8	52	175	36	.365	184	411	.226
BRADLEY, SCOTT	105	290	27	80	11	3	5	31	2	.393	15	13	.276
BRAVO, ANGEL	149	218	26	54	7	3	1	12	2	.321	20	31	.248
BREAZEALE, JIM	89	109	20	40	5	0	9	33	0	.661	16	25	.367
BRIDEWESER, JIM	329	620	79	156	22	4	6	50	6	.310	63	78	.252
BRINKMAN, CHUCK	148	267	22	46	7	0	1	12	0	.210	23	60	.172
BROHAMER, JACK	805	2500	262	613	91	12	30	227	9	.327	222	178	.245
BROWN, DICK	636	1856	175	475	62	3	62	223	7	.380	117	356	.244
BUFORD, DON	1286	4553	771	1203	157	44	93	418	200	.379	672	575	.264
BURGESS, SMOKY	1691	4471	485	1318	230	33	126	673	13	.446	477	270	.295
BUSBY, JIM	1352	4250	541	1113	162	35	48	438	97	.350	310	439	.262
CALLISON, JOHNNY	1886	6652	926	1757	321	89	226	840	74	.441	650	1064	.264
CANGELOSI, JOHN	142	440	67	103	16	3	2	32	50	.298	71	62	.234
CAREY, ANDY	938	2850	371	741	119	28	64	350	9	.396	268	389	.260
CARRASQUEL, CHICO	1325	4644	491	1229	191	29	55	474	31	.342	491	467	.258
CARREON, CAMILO	354	986	113	260	43	4	11	114	3	.349	97	117	.264
CASH, NORM	2089	6705	1046	1860	241	41	377	1103	43	.488	1043	1091	.271
CATER, DANNY	1289	4451	491	1229	191	29	66	519	26	.375	254	467	.276
CAUSEY, WAYNE	1105	3244	357	819	130	26	35	295	12	.341	390	341	.252
CAVARRETTA, PHIL	2030	6754	990	1977	347	99	95	920	65	.416	820	598	.293
CHAPMAN, BEN	1717	6478	1144	1958	407	107	90	977	287	.440	824	556	.302
CHAPPAS, HARRY	72	184	26	45	4	0	1	12	2	.283	15	26	.245
CHRISTIAN, BOB	54	147	13	33	5	0	4	19	3	.340	11	23	.224
CLARK, ALLIE	358	1021	131	267	48	4	32	149	2	.410	72	70	.262
COAN, GIL	918	2877	384	731	98	44	39	278	83	.359	232	384	.254
COGGINS, RICH	342	1083	125	287	42	13	12	90	50	.361	72	79	.265
COLAVITO, ROCKY	1841	6503	971	1730	283	21	374	1159	19	.489	951	880	.266
COLBERN, MIKE	80	224	16	58	10	2	2	28	0	.348	5	61	.259
COLEMAN, RAY	559	1729	208	446	74	33	20	199	9	.374	148	158	.258
COLUCCIO, BOB	370	1095	141	241	38	15	26	114	33	.353	128	202	.220
COURTNEY, CLINT	946	2796	260	750	126	17	38	313	3	.366	265	143	.268
COVINGTON, WES	1075	2978	355	832	128	17	131	499	7	.466	247	414	.279
CRAIG, RODNEY	135	357	46	92	25	7	3	27	7	.364	22	46	.258
CRUZ, HENRY	171	280	32	64	7	1	8	34	1	.361	25	31	.229
CRUZ, JULIO	1156	3859	557	916	113	27	23	279	343	.299	478	508	.237
CRUZ, TODD	544	1351	133	336	58	6	34	154	9	.333	59	318	.220
CUCCINELLO, TONY	1704	6184	730	1729	334	46	94	884	42	.394	579	497	.280
CULLEN, TIM	700	1761	155	387	57	9	9	134	23	.278	147	219	.220
CUNNINGHAM, JOE	1141	3362	599	980	177	26	64	436	16	.417	599	368	.291
DAVIS, TOMMY	1999	7223	811	2121	272	35	153	1052	136	.405	381	754	.294
DELSING, JIM	822	2461	322	627	112	21	40	286	15	.366	299	251	.255
DEMAESTRI, JOE	1121	3441	322	813	114	23	49	281	15	.325	168	511	.236
DENT, BUCKY	1392	4512	451	1114	169	23	40	423	17	.321	328	350	.247
DESA, JOE	35	55	11	11	2	1	0	5	0	.345	3	8	.200
DILLARD, STEVE	438	1013	148	246	50	2	13	102	6	.343	76	147	.243
DILONE, MIGUEL	722	1780	296	504	67	22	6	122	250	.339	132	178	.283
DOBY, LARRY	1533	5348	960	1515	243	52	253	969	47	.490	871	1011	.283
DOWNING, BRIAN	1586	5201	763	1382	235	17	166	734	40	.413	784	719	.266
DROPO, WALT	1288	4124	478	1113	168	22	152	704	9	.432	328	582	.270
DYBZINSKI, JERRY	463	905	109	213	32	5	5	93	32	.292	70	109	.235
DYKES, JIMMY	2282	8046	1108	2256	453	90	109	1071	70	.400	954	849	.280
EDWARDS, HANK	735	2191	285	613	116	41	51	276	2	.440	208	264	.280
EGAN, TOM	373	979	74	196	25	3	22	91	2	.299	80	336	.200
ELIA, LEE	95	212	17	43	5	2	3	25	0	.288	15	45	.203
ELLIOTT, BOB	1978	7141	1064	2061	383	94	170	1195	60	.440	967	604	.289
ENNIS, DEL	1903	7254	985	2063	258	69	288	1284	45	.472	597	719	.284
ESPOSITO, SAMMY	560	792	130	164	27	2	8	73	9	.277	145	127	.207
ESSIAN, JIM	709	1854	194	452	85	3	33	206	1	.346	231	171	.244
EWING, SAM	167	361	31	92	11	3	6	47	1	.352	28	65	.255
FAIN, FERRIS	1151	3930	595	1139	213	30	48	570	46	.396	903	261	.290
FARLEY, BOB	84	123	19	20	7	0	3	9	0	.252	30	28	.163
FISK, CARLTON	1827	6521	1003	1767	316	42	281	977	115	.462	619	1006	.271
FLETCHER, SCOTT	559	1619	218	426	75	14	11	149	33	.347	163	183	.263
FOLEY, MARVIS	203	419	37	94	10	0	12	51	0	.334	41	61	.224
FOSTER, GEORGE	1890	6739	956	1861	301	44	334	1197	50	.483	642	1358	.276
FOX, NELLIE	2367	9232	1279	2663	355	112	35	790	76	.363	719	216	.288
FRANCONA, TITO	1719	5121	650	1395	224	46	125	656	46	.403	544	694	.272
FREESE, GENE	1115	3446	429	877	161	28	115	432	51	.418	243	535	.254
FREGOSI, JIM	1902	6523	844	1726	264	78	151	706	76	.398	715	1097	.265
GAMBLE, OSCAR	1584	4502	656	1195	188	31	200	666	47	.454	610	546	.265
GARR, RALPH	1317	5108	717	1562	212	64	75	408	172	.416	246	445	.306
GILES, BRIAN	199	545	53	127	20	5	5	37	23	.407	48	109	.233
GINSBERG, JOE	695	1716	168	414	59	8	20	182	7	.320	226	135	.241
GOLDSBERRY, GORDON	217	510	78	123	20	7	6	56	2	.343	80	66	.241
GOODMAN, BILLY	1623	5644	807	1691	299	44	19	591	37	.378	669	329	.300
GRAY, LORENZO	58	106	22	22	4	0	1	4	2	.274	10	20	.208
GROTH, JOHNNY	1248	3808	480	1064	197	31	60	486	19	.395	419	329	.279
GUILLEN, OZZIE	309	1038	129	271	40	13	3	80	15	.333	24	88	.261

PLAYER	G	AB	R	H	2B	3B	HR	RBI	SB	SLG	BB	SO	AVG
GUTTERIDGE, DON	1151	4202	586	1075	200	64	39	391	95	.362	309	444	.256
HAIRSTON, JERRY	788	1568	202	408	83	6	25	185	4	.369	257	215	.260
HANSEN, RON	1384	4311	446	1007	156	17	106	501	9	.405	551	643	.234
HASSEY, RON	793	2331	249	658	121	7	50	322	5	.405	274	233	.282
HATFIELD, FRED	722	2039	259	493	67	10	25	165	15	.321	248	247	.242
HATTON, GRADY	1312	4206	562	1068	166	33	91	533	42	.374	646	430	.254
HEATH, BILL	112	199	23	47	6	1	4	13	0	.276	26	22	.236
HELD, WOODY	1390	4019	524	963	150	22	179	559	14	.421	509	944	.240
HENDERSON, KEN	1444	4553	595	1168	216	26	122	576	86	.396	589	763	.257
HERRMANN, ED	922	2729	247	654	92	4	80	320	6	.364	260	311	.240
HERSHBERGER, MIKE	1150	3572	398	900	150	22	26	344	74	.328	319	311	.252
HICKS, JIM	93	141	16	23	1	3	5	14	0	.319	18	48	.163
HICKS, JOE	212	416	41	92	11	3	12	39	1	.349	29	73	.221
HILL, DONNIE	357	1064	123	290	42	4	11	108	15	.351	55	104	.273
HILL, MARC	715	1790	144	401	62	3	34	198	1	.319	184	240	.224
HOPKINS, GAIL	514	1219	142	324	47	6	25	145	1	.376	160	83	.266
HULETT, TIM	305	927	106	227	35	9	22	81	11	.373	52	176	.245
HUNTZ, STEVE	237	636	81	131	19	1	16	60	1	.314	108	122	.206
JACKSON, RON H.	196	474	54	116	18	1	17	52	1	.395	45	119	.245
JETER, JOHNNY	336	873	108	213	27	10	18	69	29	.360	46	237	.244
JOHNSON, DARRELL	134	320	24	75	6	1	2	28	1	.278	24	39	.234
JOHNSON, DERON	1765	5941	706	1447	247	33	245	923	11	.420	706	1318	.244
JOHNSON, LAMAR	792	2631	294	755	122	12	64	381	21	.415	212	307	.287
JOHNSON, RANDY S.	101	254	26	62	10	0	10	36	0	.402	32	50	.244
JOHNSTONE, JAY	1748	4703	578	1254	215	38	102	531	50	.394	429	632	.267
JOK, STAN	12	19	4	3	0	0	1	4	0	.316	2	9	.158
JONES, CLEON	1213	4263	565	1196	183	33	93	524	91	.404	360	702	.281
JONES, DEACON	40	49	7	14	2	1	1	10	0	.429	6	8	.286
JOSEPHSON, DUANE	470	1505	147	388	58	12	23	164	5	.358	92	174	.258
KARKOVICE, RON	37	97	13	24	7	0	4	13	0	.443	9	37	.247
KELL, GEORGE	1795	6702	881	2054	385	50	78	870	51	.414	620	287	.306
KELLY, H. PAT	1385	4338	620	1147	189	76	76	418	250	.377	588	768	.264
KEMP, STEVE	1139	4006	578	1117	179	25	129	631	37	.433	570	590	.279
KENNEDY, BOB	1483	4624	514	1176	196	41	63	514	45	.355	364	443	.254
KENWORTHY, DICK	125	251	12	54	6	0	1	13	0	.295	10	42	.215
KEOUGH, JOE	332	863	95	212	26	5	9	81	9	.319	87	75	.246
KESSINGER, DON	2078	7651	899	1931	254	80	14	527	100	.312	684	759	.252
KIMM, BRUCE	186	439	35	104	19	3	1	26	5	.292	32	50	.237
KING, JIM	1125	2918	374	699	112	19	117	401	23	.411	363	401	.240
KITTLE, RON	536	1770	238	408	61	3	115	299	6	.463	157	501	.231
KLUSZEWSKI, TED	1718	5929	881	1766	290	29	279	1028	20	.498	492	365	.298
KNOOP, BOBBY	1153	3622	337	856	129	29	56	331	16	.334	305	833	.236
KOLLOWAY, DON	1079	3993	466	1081	180	30	29	393	76	.353	189	251	.271
KRESS, CHARLIE	175	466	57	116	20	1	7	52	6	.328	49	59	.249
KRESS, RED	1391	5087	691	1454	298	58	89	799	47	.420	474	453	.286
KRSNICH, ROCKY	120	275	27	59	18	1	6	38	0	.335	30	24	.215
KUNTZ, RUSTY	272	436	75	104	23	3	5	38	5	.326	58	104	.239
KUSNYER, ART	139	313	21	55	6	1	3	21	1	.230	21	61	.176
LAFRANCOIS, ROGER	8	10	1	4	1	0	0	2	0	.500	0	0	.400
LANDIS, JIM	1346	4288	625	1061	169	50	93	467	139	.375	588	767	.247
LARUSSA, TONY	132	176	15	35	5	2	0	7	1	.250	23	37	.199
LAW, RUDY	749	2421	379	656	101	37	18	199	228	.366	184	210	.271
LAW, VANCE	724	2268	279	566	108	19	41	257	23	.368	246	361	.250
LEFLORE, RON	1099	4458	731	1283	172	57	59	353	455	.446	363	888	.288
LEMON, CHET	1586	5150	731	1429	302	53	166	666	53	.451	526	745	.277
LEMON, JIM	1010	3445	446	901	120	35	164	529	13	.460	363	787	.262
LENHARDT, DON	481	1481	192	401	64	9	61	239	13	.450	235	235	.271
LEON, EDDIE	601	1862	165	440	51	10	29	159	7	.313	156	358	.236
LEPCIO, TED	729	2092	233	512	91	11	69	251	11	.398	210	471	.245
LITTLE, BRYAN	293	846	120	212	35	5	4	75	8	.314	114	68	.251
LOLICH, RON	87	228	20	48	9	0	4	23	0	.303	11	49	.211
LOLLAR, SHERMAN	1752	5351	623	1415	244	14	155	808	20	.402	671	453	.264

PLAYER	G	AB	R	H	2B	3B	HR	RBI	SB	SLG	BB	SO	AVG
LONG, JEOFF	56	83	5	16		0	1		0	.241	10	34	.193
LOPEZ, AL	1950	5916	613	1547	206	42	52	652	46	.337	561	538	.261
LOVIGLIO, JAY	46	82	17	10				4	5	.192		17	.234
LUZINSKI, GREG	1821	6505	880	1795	344	24	307	1128	37	.478	845	1495	.276
LYONS, STEVE	234	649	82	154	23	6	4	50	16	.335	51	111	.249
LYTTLE, JIM	391	710	71	176	37	5	9	70	4	.352	61	139	.248
MAHONEY, JIM	120	210	32	48	4	1	4	15	1	.314	47	47	.229
MAJESKI, HANK	1069	3421	404	956	181	27	57	501	10	.398	299	260	.279
MARSH, FREDDIE	465	1236	148	296	43	8	10	96	13	.311	125	171	.239
MARSHALL, WILLARD	1246	4233	583	1160	163	39	130	604	14	.423	458	219	.274
MARTIN, J.C.	908	2189	189	487	82	12	32	230	9	.315	201	299	.222
MASI, PHIL	1229	3468	420	917	164	31	47	417	45	.370	410	311	.264
MATIAS, JOHN	58	117	7	22	6	0	1	6	1	.256	3	22	.188
MAXWELL, CHARLIE	1133	3245	478	856	110	26	148	532	18	.451	545	545	.264
MAY, CARLOS	1165	4120	544	1127	172	23	90	536	85	.392	512	565	.274
MAY, MILT	1192	3693	313	971	147	11	77	443	1	.371	305	361	.263
MAYE, LEE	1288	4048	533	1109	190	39	94	419	59	.410	282	481	.274
MCCRAW, TOM	1468	3956	484	972	150	42	75	404	143	.362	332	544	.246
MCGHEE, ED	196	505	59	124	14	5	3	43	11	.311	61	61	.246
MCKINNEY, RICH	341	886	79	199	28	2	20	100	4	.328	77	124	.225
MELE, SAM	1046	3437	406	916	168	39	80	544	15	.408	311	342	.267
MELTON, BILL	1144	3972	499	1004	162	9	160	591	23	.419	479	669	.253
METKOVICH, GEORGE	1055	3585	476	934	167	36	47	373	61	.367	307	359	.261
MEYER, BILLY	113	301	15	71	7	3	1	21	3	.289	15	25	.236
MICHAELS, CASS	1288	4367	508	1142	147	46	53	501	64	.353	566	406	.262
MINOSO, MINNIE	1835	6597	1136	1963	336	83	186	1023	205	.459	814	584	.298
MIRANDA, WILLIE	824	1914	176	423	50	14	6	132	13	.271	165	250	.221
MOLINARO, BOB	401	803	106	212	25	11	14	90	45	.375	65	57	.264
MOORE, JUNIOR	289	774	83	204	20	7	7	73	7	.335	62	71	.264
MORALES, RICH	480	1053	81	205	26	3	6	64	7	.242	95	159	.195
MORMAN, RUSS	49	159	18	40	4	1	4	17	1	.358	16	36	.252
MORRISON, JIM	884	2744	302	730	140	14	97	351	40	.433	174	457	.266
MOSES, WALLY	2012	7356	1114	2138	435	110	89	679	174	.416	821	411	.291
MOSS, LES	824	2234	210	552	75	4	63	276	5	.369	282	316	.247
MUELLER, DON	1245	4364	499	1292	139	37	65	520	11	.390	167	146	.296
MULLEAVY, GREG	79	292	28	76	14	5	0	28	5	.342	20	23	.260
MULLINS, FRAN	117	172	17	36	12	1	2	13	0	.314	18	37	.209
MURPHY, DANNY	117	130	18	23	5	1	4	13	3	.323	11	41	.177
MUSER, TONY	663	1268	123	329	41	9	7	117	14	.323	95	138	.259
NAHRODNY, BILL	308	844	74	203	41	3	25	109	0	.385	56	118	.241
NASH, COTTON	13	16	2	3	0	0	0	2	0	.188	3	3	.188
NELSON, ROCKY	620	1394	186	347	61	14	31	173	7	.379	130	94	.249
NIARHOS, GUS	315	691	114	174	26	6	1	59	6	.308	153	56	.252
NICHOLS, REID	463	1013	134	269	55	6	18	111	25	.385	85	136	.266
NICHOLSON, DAVE	538	1419	184	301	32	12	61	179	6	.381	219	573	.212
NIEMAN, BOB	1113	3452	455	1018	180	32	125	544	10	.474	244	512	.295
NORDBROOK, TIM	128	169	27	30	8	1	0	2	1	.195	35	58	.178
NORDHAGEN, WAYNE	502	1423	147	401	77	8	39	205	4	.429	54	162	.282
NORMAN, BILL	37	103	13	21	5	1	1	8	0	.272	6	13	.204
NORTHEY, RON	1084	3172	385	874	172	28	108	513	7	.450	297	276	.276
NYMAN, CHRIS	49	93	18	24	4	0	2	6	3	.333	11	16	.258
NYMAN, NYLS	120	357	43	85	9	8	2	33	12	.303	38	38	.238
O'BRIEN, SYD	378	1052	135	242	35	8	24	100	5	.347	60	155	.230
O'MALLEY, TOM	316	937	88	238	48	5	9	95	4	.333	104	116	.254
O'NEILL, STEVE	1586	4795	448	1259	248	34	13	537	30	.337	592	283	.263
ORTA, JORGE	1734	5779	730	1610	263	63	128	741	79	.412	497	707	.279
PACIOREK, TOM	1365	4061	488	1145	229	30	83	491	55	.414	244	685	.282
PAVLETICH, DON	536	1373	163	349	73	8	46	193	2	.420	148	237	.254
PERCONTE, JACK	409	1368	185	373	46	16	2	72	76	.334	138	113	.273
PHILLIPS, DAVE	1904	6296	789	1700	276	72	84	729	102	.377	596	551	.270
PHILLIPS, BUBBA	1062	3278	348	835	135	62	62	356	35	.358	182	413	.255
PILARCIK, AL	668	1614	205	413	66	7	22	143	41	.346	185	150	.256

PLAYER	G	AB	R	H	2B	3B	HR	RBI	SB	SLG	BB	SO	AVG
WAGNER, LEON	1352	4426	636	1202	150	15	211	669	54	.455	435	656	.272
WALKER, DIXIE	1905	6740	1037	2064	376	96	105	1023	59	.437	817	325	.306
WALKER, GREG	506	1649	211	453	95	16	73	280	16	.485	138	270	.275
WARD, PETE	973	3060	345	776	136	17	98	427	20	.405	371	539	.254
WASHINGTON, CLAUDELL	1529	5488	762	1524	275	61	130	665	270	.421	386	1029	.278
WEIS, AL	800	1578	195	346	45	11	7	115	55	.275	117	299	.219
WILLIAMS, WALT	842	2373	284	640	106	33	40	173	24	.365	126	211	.270
WILSON, BILL D.	224	654	87	145	23	1	32	77	2	.407	72	136	.222
WRIGHT, TOM	341	685	75	175	28	11	6	99	3	.355	76	123	.255
YORK, RUDY	1603	5891	876	1621	291	52	277	1152	38	.483	791	867	.275
ZARILLA, AL	1120	3535	507	975	186	43	61	456	33	.405	415	382	.276
ZERNIAL, GUS	1234	4131	572	1093	159	22	237	776	15	.486	383	755	.265
ZISK, RICHIE	1453	5144	681	1477	245	26	207	792	8	.466	533	910	.287

PLAYER	G	AB	R	H	2B	3B	HR	RBI	SB	SLG	BB	SO	AVG
POWELL, LEROY	2	0	0	0	0	0	0	0	0	—	0	0	—
PRUITT, RON	341	795	88	214	28	4	12	92	9	.360	93	90	.269
PRYOR, GREG	789	1883	204	471	85	9	14	146	11	.327	104	185	.250
QUALLS, JIM	63	139	13	31	5	3	0	10	3	.302	2	16	.223
QUIRK, JAMIE	534	1188	100	286	58	4	23	125	3	.354	63	228	.241
RADER, DOUG	1465	5186	631	1302	245	39	155	722	37	.403	528	1057	.251
REDUS, GARY	459	1516	284	376	80	22	42	141	171	.413	219	333	.248
REICHARDT, RICK	997	3307	391	864	109	22	116	445	2	.445	263	672	.261
RICHARD, LEE	239	492	71	103	12	6	2	29	12	.270	33	77	.209
RICHARDS, PAUL	523	1417	140	321	51	11	15	155	4	.301	157	149	.227
RICKERT, MARV	402	1149	139	284	45	19	19	145	4	.352	88	161	.247
RIDDLE, JOHNNY	98	214	18	51	4	1	0	11	0	.266	13	19	.238
RIVERA, JIM	1171	3552	503	911	155	56	83	422	160	.402	365	523	.256
ROBINSON, EDDIE	1314	4279	545	1145	171	24	172	723	10	.439	520	359	.268
ROBINSON, FLOYD	1012	3284	458	929	140	36	67	426	42	.409	408	282	.283
RODRIGUEZ, AURELIO	2017	6611	612	1570	287	46	124	648	35	.351	324	943	.237
ROMANO, JOHNNY	905	2767	355	706	112	10	129	417	7	.443	414	504	.255
ROOF, PHIL	857	2151	190	463	69	13	43	210	11	.319	184	504	.215
ROSELLI, BOB	68	114	8	25	7	1	2	10	0	.351	12	31	.219
ROYSTER, JERRY	1287	3910	518	979	149	33	33	324	185	.331	382	486	.250
RYAN, CONNIE	1184	3982	535	988	181	42	56	381	69	.357	518	514	.248
SADOWSKI, BOB F.	184	329	38	73	9	3	3	46	3	.331	33	63	.222
SALAZAR, LUIS	651	2136	232	565	79	24	39	232	103	.379	84	358	.265
SANTO, RON	2243	8143	1138	2254	365	67	342	1331	35	.464	1108	1343	.277
SAWATSKI, CARL	633	1449	133	351	46	5	58	213	2	.401	191	251	.242
SCHAFFER, JIMMIE	304	574	53	128	28	3	11	56	3	.340	49	127	.223
SHARP, BILL	397	1104	122	281	52	8	3	95	14	.341	75	109	.255
SIEVERS, ROY	1887	6387	945	1703	292	42	318	1147	14	.475	841	920	.267
SILVESTRI, KEN	102	203	26	44	11	1	5	25	0	.355	31	41	.217
SIMPSON, HARRY	888	2829	343	752	101	41	73	381	17	.408	271	429	.266
SKINNER, JOEL	185	450	38	108	15	2	6	46	2	.322	28	116	.240
SKIZAS, LOU	239	725	80	196	27	4	30	86	8	.443	50	37	.270
SKOWRON, BILL	1658	5547	681	1566	243	53	211	888	16	.459	383	870	.282
SMALLEY, ROY JR.	1543	5348	713	1369	228	24	155	660	25	.395	735	856	.256
SMITH, AL	1517	5357	843	1458	258	46	164	676	67	.429	674	768	.272
SMITH, CHARLIE	771	2484	228	594	83	18	69	281	7	.370	130	565	.239
SNYDER, RUSS	1365	3631	450	984	150	38	42	319	58	.363	294	438	.271
SODERHOLM, ERIC	894	2894	402	764	120	14	102	383	15	.421	295	359	.264
SOUCHOCK, STEVE	473	1227	163	313	58	11	50	186	15	.457	88	164	.255
SPENCE, BOB	72	183	13	37	5	1	4	19	0	.306	16	47	.202
SPENCER, JIM	1553	4908	541	1227	179	27	146	599	11	.387	407	582	.250
SPIEZIO, ED	554	1544	126	367	56	10	39	174	6	.355	135	245	.238
SQUIRES, MIKE	777	1580	210	411	53	6	6	141	45	.318	143	108	.260
STAEHLE, MARV	185	455	53	94	12	1	1	33	4	.244	54	35	.207
STANKY, EDDIE	1259	4301	811	1154	185	35	29	364	48	.348	996	374	.268
STEGMAN, DAVE	171	320	39	66	10	2	8	32	4	.325	31	55	.206
STEIN, BILL	959	2811	268	751	122	18	44	311	16	.370	186	413	.267
STEPHENS, GENE	964	1913	283	460	78	15	37	207	25	.355	233	322	.240
STEPHENS, VERN	1720	6497	1001	1859	307	42	247	1174	25	.460	692	685	.286
STEWART, ED	773	2041	288	547	96	32	32	260	29	.393	252	157	.268
STILLMAN, ROYLE	89	155	19	33	7	1	3	15	2	.305	21	28	.213
STROUD, ED	529	1353	209	320	37	28	14	100	72	.336	129	224	.237
SUTHERLAND, LEO	45	101	15	25	3	0	0	5	2	.277	4	12	.248
TANNER, CHUCK	396	885	98	231	39	5	21	105	6	.388	82	93	.261
TIPTON, JOE	417	1117	116	264	36	5	29	125	2	.355	186	142	.236
TOLLESON, WAYNE	568	1700	217	433	48	14	1	93	96	.312	146	256	.255
TORGESON, EARL	1668	4969	848	1318	215	46	149	740	133	.417	980	653	.265
TORRES, RUSTY	654	1314	159	279	45	9	35	126	13	.334	164	246	.212
TURNER, JERRY	733	1742	222	448	73	5	45	238	45	.272	159	245	.257
VARNEY, PETE	69	190	18	47	7	1	5	15	2	.374	10	47	.247
VOSS, BILL	475	1177	119	267	29	10	19	127	15	.317	117	167	.227